JESSIE JULIET KNOX,
In Chinese Costume.

In the House of the Tiger

By
JESSIE JULIET KNOX

Author of
"Little Almond Blossoms."

Cincinnati:
JENNINGS AND GRAHAM

New York:
EATON AND MAINS

COPYRIGHT, 1911, BY
JENNINGS AND GRAHAM

WITH DEEPEST LOVE AND ADMIRATION
I DEDICATE THIS BOOK TO
MY FRIEND

Donaldine M. Cameron

SUPERINTENDENT OF THE OCCIDENTAL MISSION HOUSE
SAN FRANCISCO, CALIFORNIA

CONTENTS

LIST OF ILLUSTRATIONS

LIST OF ILLUSTRATIONS

CHAPTER ONE

THE MESSAGE OF THE LANTERNS

"HY? WHY?"

The dear little slave girl, Ah Ching, had asked this question many times, and, somehow, to-night she felt as though the answer were about to come. She was so tired of this upside-down place, and the upside-downness of everything in it, but knew not how to change it. In the big world somewhere there must be a place where things were right side up; but where?

She could only ask the question of the heavy baby for whom it was her duty to care, but the poor baby was a little captive, too, and could but blink its almond eyes in reply. Whence this child had come Ah Ching knew not, nor indeed cared. She only knew it was too heavy for her poor, aching back.

Somehow the great shining lanterns on all the Chinese balconies seemed alive to-night, and surely, ah, surely, beckoned to the *mooie jai* (slave girl).

The huge "lanterns of the Dragon" were even more attractive to her than to those who were free and inhabited the upper world. To one who had always lived in an underground home, mysterious with many windings, that same upper world appeared very charming, as indeed it really was, in this fair country.

You may not believe it, but these big lanterns sometimes talked to Ah Ching, and on this eventful night, when the picturesque and crooked streets were aglow with their light, and thousands of happy and gayly dressed people of all nations thronged past

"She only knew it was too heavy for her poor, aching back."

the unnoticed grating in the cellar window, knowing not that a pale face peeped from its tiny opening, the lanterns were talking to her in the magical voices that good fairies always use. As they talked, her child's heart was filled with bright images, and vague, mysterious dreams—dreams of a place where things were right, and people were warm and happy and free.

To hear and understand the message of the lanterns one must have the pure heart and the simple faith of a child, for only to such do the fairies talk.

And the bright globes said, as the salt breeze from the ocean blew them from side to side, "*Seung loy nee do guong deung, se lah, 'ngau ho, mooie jai.*" (Come up into the light, my dear little slave!)

How alluring it sounded to a child in the dark, for when one is a Chinese slave girl, and worth three thousand dollars in gold, one is not apt to run about in the light. To do that would mean to run the risk of being seen by certain "white devils," and of being "rescued" by the sweet-faced, but determined, lady who makes it her life work to keep watch and ward over the traffic in Chinese slave girls, in the City of the Golden West.

Ah Ching had heard of this lady, but knew not whether to love or hate her, as some of the Chinese men called her "*Lo Foo*" (The Tiger). Well might they give her that name, for many times she had snatched from them their innocent prey.

Somehow, Ah Ching wished they would not call the lady by such a name, because a tiger is cruel, and does not know love and tenderness, and she could not believe that one who was not afraid of the wicked masters, but who would face death itself to rescue a timid slave, was cruel. No! Long and often had she pondered upon this subject, and always something seemed to tell her that the lady was kind and noble and true.

O, why could she not be free? Why could she not walk the streets and breathe the air, now laden with the fragrance of the sacred *hong fah* (almond flower) and the incense burning ever for the gods? The eternal WHY of things tired her brain, and she laid her head upon the hard shelf under the window grating.

Strange it was that, although her eyes were closed, she could still see the lanterns, and they had gone up into the sky and resolved themselves into one huge interrogation point. And then—and then, from out the very largest one, came, like a shooting star, a great yellow Tiger, with half-closed eyes—yet she did not cry out; she did not even feel afraid. How very strange!

Nearer and nearer came the Tiger, until Ah Ching could feel its breath, and now all fear was gone. She put out her hand and touched it, and she heard it say in musical tones, "*Samen jai* (child), do not fear me. I am nothing but love and tenderness for poor slave girls, and instead of harming you I would save you."

"O dear, good *Lo Foo* (Tiger), do let me come up into the light!" gasped the *mooie jai*.

"Little one, I will!" the Tiger purred softly, and vanished into the very heart of the radiant lantern.

Do you say she was dreaming? No, Ah Ching *knew*. It was *real*. She also knew why she was thus favored of the gods. Was it not because—whisper it softly that the idols may not hear—when the old hag who guarded her had believed her to be offering her devotions to the ugly paper god on the wall, and the *Jov Gwoon* (kitchen god) over the great stone oven, she was in reality praying—to the lanterns. No one but the lanterns knew this, and no one need ever know.

The young girl had no faith in these images anyhow, and away back in the recesses of her Chinese brain she believed that they were devils, and in league with the old woman who guarded her, and the sleek, silk-gowned highbinder who owned her.

But her lanterns! O, they were good spirits who came to her aid and answered her innocent petitions, and no one knew. She believed with the faith of a child—why, she knew not—that some day they would come and take her away from this life of bondage, away from the cruel words, the blows, and the drudgery, and that somehow she would be lifted "into the light."

"Perhaps there is a place for me out there in the big world—perhaps there is some one there who would love me, and be kind to me. O, if I could only get out, I would help all the other poor slaves to be free."

And the great interrogation point seemed

to grow and scintillate on the sky, until suddenly the lanterns changed to dainty ladies who smiled, and reached down soft hands to the child, saying, "Come up into the light, my dear little slave!" when—the harsh voice of the old woman fell rudely upon her ear, and the sweet vision vanished.

"What do you mean by doing nothing, you worthless slave? Come quickly, and put the offerings before the gods!"

With a heavy heart, the drowsy child slipped back into the semi-darkness of the place, whose misty corners, she had been told, were filled with bad spirits, waiting to catch her if she faltered or were at all remiss in her attentions to the staring gods on the wall.

Gliding through the devious ways of the underground place, which was filled with the fumes of opium, she caught a fragment of conversation between her master and another highbinder. The stranger was young and

"Come up into the light, my dear little slave!"

handsome, and had a kind voice, and her child's intuition told her that he could not be very bad at heart, even though he did belong to the order. Perhaps he had been compelled to join, for, if one could judge by a voice and a face, surely this young man would not kill.

They did not know she heard, for she only peeped through a tiny crevice in the door, and crouching there, with her heart beating so loudly under the dark *sohm* (blouse) that she feared they might hear it, she caught the words uttered by the young man.

"To-morrow is 'lantern day.' Why not let the *mooie jai* go out upon the streets? There will be the parade at night, you know, and—poor child—once a year is not much."

It seemed to the tense little figure a lifetime before her master replied, but in that lifetime she had breathed a soft prayer: "O, good *joss*—No, no, not that—O, good Lanterns of the Dragon—*gowsi oon loong* (beautiful lanterns) let me go! only let me go! Just once to be free, and to see the lanterns, and walk with the people, and then—and then—"

Her owner was speaking now, and very reluctantly, it is true, giving his consent, on condition that the girl be well guarded by the old woman.

Ah! now her heart was light. Willingly would she set food before the gods, and discharge her duties.

The process seemed a strange one, but not so to Ah Ching, because to her it was all so familiar. She was hungry, and felt a strong desire to eat the *fon* (rice) and *shew yuk* (pork) as she placed it in steaming bowls before the idols. The tiny bowls, not much larger than thimbles, were filled with *jow* (wine) for the supposed use of the *joss*. She could see that he never ate any of these things, and it always seemed to her such a waste.

One time when she had ventured to make a remark to this effect, she had received a blow, and had been told that the gods ate only the delicate portions which the human eye was too gross to see. She had never dared speak of it again, but in her heart she knew it was not true, for paper gods could neither see nor hear nor feel.

She would rather worship the big round lantern, because there was a god in it. She knew, for IT had spoken to her many times.

As this was the last night of the old year, there was much to be done in the way of worship. Many and various had been the Chinese delicacies prepared for this occasion, and it was the duty of the slave to place them all upon the table, in front of the gods and goddesses.

The huge Chinese lemons and tiny mandarin oranges were piled in pyramids, and the bowls of rice and sweets arranged in a way calculated to please the gods.

She artistically filled the bowls with Chinese lilies, poking her little nose into their fragrant hearts the while, and fastening red paper around the stems, to frighten away evil spirits.

Next, taking a piece of Chinese money with a square hole in the center, she fastened it on the end of a chop stick, set it in a bowl of incense ashes, and placed on top of it a curious punk or incense coil, which looked like a curled up snake. Lighting this, she proceeded to worship the gods, while the smoke wreaths almost concealed her. Ah Ching bowed her head many times, repeating strange heathen incantations. A strip of matting was kept on the floor in front of the altar, and at each *kow-tow* (bowing the head) her forehead came in contact with it. She closed her eyes that she might not see the images, for she feared they would discern that it was not to them she was addressing her prayers.

As soon as possible she ceased her devotions, as she was weary and wished to retire to think over all the bright possibilities of the morrow.

While making her preparations she heard a noise which seemed to be at the trap door in the roof, right over her bed. Suddenly this door opened just a little way, and from the opening dropped a package. Such a thing was so unheard of and out of the ordinary that she felt startled, and almost afraid to touch it. It looked innocent enough, however, and childish curiosity, mingled with a vague hope of something pleasant, caused her at last to untie the red silk string of the New Year, and there—O, joy unbelievable—was a *lantern*; such a beauty, of the most delicately painted silken gauze.

"Whose can it be?" she wondered. "It must have dropped by mistake." Just then she saw a card, and on it, written in large letters:

FOR THE LITTLE SLAVE GIRL, AH CHING.

A big lump came into her throat and her eyes filled with tears. Who could have done it? Who? Suddenly a thought came to her. Could it be? Ah, well, it did not matter who had dropped the lantern through the trap door. It was surely the "lantern gods" who sent it. No one else could have inscribed upon it such precious wishes for long life and happiness. No one else would care. No one had ever cared. Now she, too, could "burn a lantern before the heavens!" Her heart was so full of joy that she felt as if she must fly right through the roof, far from bondage and care, away to the bright land where lived the lantern gods and goddesses, and where the air

"The rich balcony across the street."

was always filled with the fragrance of *suey seen fah* (Chinese lilies) "angel flowers in water," and *hong fah* (almond blossoms).

Hugging her treasure to her heart, she soon fell asleep, only to dream of soft, yellow tigers who spoke to her words of tenderness, and looked lovingly at her from half-shut eyes of golden gray.

When she awoke it was the great day of the "lantern feast." It was the day when some of even the slave girls were allowed to walk the streets, trying to imagine for a few hours that they were free.

Hastily glancing from the latticed window, she found that the sun was shining, and that, therefore, the gods were propitious. She saw, also, on the rich balcony across the street—the other highbinder!

He seemed to be looking at her window, and, when he had caught a glimpse of her face, called out in cheery tones, "*Ho sun, mooie jai, 'Ngau seung nay gom yat oi gau ho yat.*" (Good morning, my little slave girl. I hope you will have a good time to-day.) His voice had such a familiar and kindly tone that the tight strings of her heart seemed to relax, while her eyes filled with tears, and she knew, she *knew* that the gods of the Lantern had sent her a *pong yow* (good friend)—a highbinder, it is true, but one with love, and not hate, in his heart. Then it seemed to her that he turned and said something to the big lanterns, and that they swayed nearer to him in reply.

No longer did she feel lonely or unhappy. What if the old hag did beat her? All the time the girl would know, away down in her heart, that she had a friend, and the highbinder and the lanterns would know, too.

The *ah mo* (old woman) questioned her as to where she had obtained the pretty lantern, but could elicit only the reply, "It came from the gods." Thinking that perhaps some of the many opium smokers who frequented the place had given it to the child, she allowed the matter to pass without further inquiry. In the girl's heart was a great fear that it would be taken from her, but, strangely enough, it was not.

To tell the truth, Ah Mo was afraid to touch this thing which had appeared so mysteriously. Her superstitious heart suggested that it might be a "devil lantern." To her this child had ever been an enigma, and she had never in the least understood the depths of the little one's nature.

Ah Ching had always been passive under the cruel blows, and no reproach had escaped her, save that which came from the pleading eyes. Once, only once, had she burst forth like a young fury, her eyes blazing and hands clenched, and had said to the old hag:

"I am a friend of all the devils, and some day, when you are beating me, I will speak one word to them, and they will strike you dead."

Until the dawn, Ah Ching clasped closely her heaven-sent treasure—the magic dawn of the day more wonderful to her than any day that had ever gone before.

The "feast of the lanterns" was the all-important event of the Chinese New Year. On this occasion, and in fact for many days previous, the shops were crowded with an interested, chattering mass of celestials, buying lanterns of all descriptions, ranging from the cheap paper ones to the wonderful creations of silk and gauze with rare paintings thereon. Many of them were quite intricate, containing ingenious mechanisms. They were round, flat, square, thin, big, and little. Some rolled on the ground, like balls of fire. Some represented children or animals, and upon some were painted the tender and loving *Kwan Yum* (mother goddess) with a child in her arms.

When at last the protecting shadows fell upon the place, Ah Ching's heart grew light. In all the homes of the great Chinese quarter of San Francisco there was rejoicing amongst rich and poor alike.

The high-caste ladies peeped down from their lofty balconies, where many expensive red candles burned for the *joss*, and even the poor ones in the cellar and tenement had their bowls of punk lighted outside the door.

The wonderful "parade of the dragon" was to take place early in the evening, so that there might be plenty of time left for the theater and other interesting entertainments.

With trembling fingers the little slave at last lighted her wonderful lantern, and hung it outside where passers-by could see its charm. Perhaps it might even send a comforting ray of light to some other miserable slave down in a cellar, or up next the roof.

How joyful it looked, swaying gently, and shining with a tender radiance.

At last the offerings had been renewed before the gods; fresh punks, big and little, had been lighted, and were burning steadily, even under tables and beds, as no place must be left for the entrance of an evil spirit.

And now came a perfect heathen uproar! It heralded the approach of the great procession of the dragon. There was a deafening roar of fireworks, and much clanging of the brazen *tom-toms*.

Many of the women and girls were not allowed to be on the street at the time of the parade, but were expected to see that the incense was kept burning and to set fire to a paper boat of "mock money," consisting of squares of light brown paper, with gold and silver spots in the center. This was thrown blazing in front of each door, just as the dragon reached that spot, and a lighted bunch of firecrackers was also hurled out.

Unless one had experienced this, it would be difficult to imagine the ear-splitting noise and the smoke caused by such continuous homage to the gods. It would almost seem as if the gods as well as the devils would be frightened at all the din.

When the big squirming dragon arrived, Ah Ching would have felt very timid had she not seen the feet of dozens of real men sticking out from under it. She knew then that it was only make-believe.

At last came the supreme moment, and Ah Mo said they would start. Who could dream what this meant for Ah Ching? It was the first time since she came here that she had been permitted to go upon the street.

How intoxicating was the first breath of pure air which caressed her face, and the fresh breeze which seemed to tell of freedom.

How gay the shop windows, and how still more enchanting were the dainty Chinese ladies and girls. Even those of high-caste were there, toddling on their tiny "bound" feet, and, like this poor slave, rejoicing at their few short hours of freedom.

Red, the joy color, was everywhere: red candles, red lanterns, red papers pasted over all the doors, and joy's red roses flamed in the faces of all the women and girls that night.

Far up on lonely balconies might be seen those who were not so fortunate as to be free, even for one night, and they gazed wistfully down at the happy crowd, sometimes dropping almond petals and sweetmeats upon the heads of the passers-by.

At many doors people were gathered in groups, trying to guess the riddles on some of the lanterns. All this was of the most intense interest to Ah Ching, and although a thought of what it would mean to leave it all and go back to her cellar home did flit through the girl's mind, she bravely put it away, and breathed: "O, good lanterns, let me be happy once! let me believe I am not a slave—let me believe I am free!"

She gazed intently upward at the great lanterns glowing everywhere. Ah Mo also gazed upward. And her mind must have been gazing too—at any rate, she did not see an open cellar door which yawned before her. So, ere the child had time to note what was taking place, the old woman had disappeared in the darkness below.

Before Ah Ching could cry out, she felt her hand taken, and herself being hurried around a corner and on to another street. Feeling frightened, she glanced up, and straight into the eyes of—the friend the lanterns had sent!

"Little one," he murmured, "the gods have set you free! Come with me!"

Now all fear was gone, and she seemed to have wings, as she tripped along and entered a closed carriage, which, by some mysterious means, stood waiting.

The young highbinder spoke into the carriage window, saying, "Here she is! I give her into your care. . . . Good-by, little one. I will come to visit you, some day."

The child's eyes filled with tears, and she could not speak. As she stepped into the darkness of the carriage she thought one of the big lanterns swayed down to her and said:

"Come up into the light, my dear little slave girl!"

Although she could not see the face, the arms in the carriage were arms of love. She did not know to whom they belonged until she at last found herself in a big bright place full of girls, once slaves like herself, but now beaming and happy. Every one was saying, "*Gong hay fot choy, Ah Mooie!*" (Happy New Year, little sister!)

Something seemed to whisper to her a delightful secret, and as she turned, and looked into the gold-gray eyes, and walked straight into the tender arms, she knew at last that she was in—The House of the Tiger.

CHAPTER TWO

GOOD LITTLE MOON

ALL the girls wished to talk to Ah Ching at the same time, Chinese fashion. She would have enjoyed hearing every word each of them said, but that was impossible. Somehow, she did not feel timid, because there was such a bond between them all, and all had passed through similar experiences.

Among the many maidens in the large room she felt particularly drawn to a dear little moon-faced tot who was kneeling on a stool with a book before her, and a chubby forefinger pointing to something on the open page.

"What is that baby doing here?" she asked. "Surely she can not have been a

"A dear little moon-faced tot."

slave." One of the older girls replied: "Yes —young as she is, the child, too, has had her sad story. Would you like to hear it?"

"'*Ngau seung teung*" (I would like to hear it), replied Ah Ching, and the child, who was called *Ah Yute Ho Jai* (good little moon) from her resemblance to that sacred orb, brought her little stool, and tenderly clung to the trembling fingers of the newly-rescued one, while the older girl told the story.

Yute Ho Jai was born in China. She was happy because she was only a baby, and had never known anything to make her unhappy.

As her mother had died soon after her birth, she had never known the sweetness of a mother's love, and her father had always left her to her own devices.

One day, while playing with her toy pagoda on the steps of her home, she was startled by hearing some one address her. She did not like the voice, and still less did she like the face, when she glanced up.

The words were spoken by an old woman who was fat and ugly, and had an evil squint in one of her eyes.

"*Hola! Ma*" (are you good?), little moon-flower?" she questioned; "How beautiful you are!"

"Would you like to go with me to the pretty *joss*-house (temple) and pray to the honorable *joss*?" she craved.

"No—no—I no likee," responded the frightened child. "I likee stay here with my pagoda; I no *sabê* (understand) *joss*."

Just then her father appeared on the scene, and the child, baby though she was, saw the old hag hand him a piece of pretty yellow money; but she did not understand. How could she, when she was so young, and knew nothing of the big world and its wicked ways? How could she know that her dainty and cream-tinted babyhood would bring a big price away across the ocean in the city of San Francisco, where Chinese slave girls were in such demand?

"Come and go with me, little blossom," coaxed the old woman. "I will take you to see beautiful things, and you will be very happy."

But the child refused to stir until so ordered by her unnatural father; then, as a Chinese child knows not the name of disobedience, she went—but not to the temple, to see the "honorable *joss*." Ah, no! the old hag did not include the gods in her plans.

The little one was now crying pitifully, and clinging in desperation to her pagoda, so the *ah mo* thrust her into a cellar, gave her some rice, and put her to bed, where she soon forgot her sorrows in the deep sleep of childhood.

It was still dark when she was rudely

awakened, and told to get up. Another bowl of rice and a cup of tea were given her, and out again they started.

She was afraid, for she felt alone and unprotected, and already hated the old woman with the true and unerring instinct of a child. On and on trudged the baby feet. She was so tired, and it was so dark and cold. How she longed for her little cot at home, but for the child there was nothing but to obey.

The old woman jerked her arm roughly, and made her walk so quickly that it seemed as though she would die.

At last they reached the big water.

What could it mean?

Could the whole world be turning to water?

She had never seen this before, although she had lived in Hong Kong ever since she was born.

What could those big houses be, out on

the water—those things that whistled and screamed in such a terrifying way?

The *ah mo*, however, did not care how terrifying it was, or how the timid child pulled back and cried to go home. She only remembered that she had just purchased for ten dollars something that she could sell for two thousand, and gold was her god.

"If you cry out or speak one word I will put you down in the water, where the sea dragon will eat you up," muttered the hag as she pulled the child along over the gangplank, and into the big ship.

Yute Ho Jai was mute and pale with terror. No need to rebel, no need to wonder why, for, child though she was, she realized that the duty of a Chinese girl is to submit to anything, at any and all times.

Four long weeks they were on the terrible water. For several days the child was quite ill, and the old woman had to care for her, as she did not wish to lose this valuable bit of celestial merchandise.

While the *ah mo* was planning what she would do with the two thousand dollars the rich highbinder was to pay her on receipt of the child, the great ship steamed into the harbor of San Francisco, and her wicked heart filled with joy. Grasping the child, she quickly walked the gangplank, thinking to herself: "Soon the danger will be over; soon I shall have the money in my hands."

But it is not such an easy matter for passengers from the Orient to land secretly, as there are people who keep themselves well informed of the arrival of the steamers. They have a purpose in so doing. Thus it chanced that when baby Yute Ho Jai's feet had touched Californian soil, and her dirty, tear-stained face was looking about her in childish wonder and affright, a sweet, but very determined-looking American lady with a distinguishing lock of white in her brown hair stepped quickly forward and took the child's hand, while a man, who happened to be a United States officer and interpreter, spoke in Chinese to the old woman, saying, "*Nay gau samen jai bene 'ngau neh?*" (Who is this child?)

"*Kooie hi 'ngau sieun mo to dow low mo geh*" (She is my orphan grandchild), replied the old woman, with furtive glances at the white lady, wondering the while if the big policeman whom she saw at a little distance could have anything to do with these people.

"I had to go over to China to get her," she resumed, "and I am going to raise her."

The wicked woman's face belied her words, however. Upon being cross-questioned by the interpreter her recital became so mixed up that it was soon found she was telling nothing but lies, and not very clever ones at that.

Dr. Gardiner, the interpreter, was well versed in the slave girl question, and it was not easy to deceive him.

As the old woman's vision saw the coveted thousands slipping from her grasp, she threw aside the mask and showed her real nature. She began to use vile language, and tried to take the child forcibly from her protector. It was then she discovered that the big policeman really did have some connection with this affair, for at the sound of the police whistle which the American lady always carried, he was at her side in an instant.

"This child is a prisoner of the United States. As such she will be cared for by us," he said; and there was no mistaking his meaning.

Those were big words for a child, and "Good Little Moon" did not understand them, even when translated into Chinese. She could only read, as children and dogs will, the faces of those around her. With a child's quick intuition, she knew that the tables were turned, and that the gentle lady and the big policeman were her friends. She clung tightly to the protecting hand of the one who had saved her from a life worse than she would ever realize.

When the old woman learned that she was not to be left in the detention shed with the rest of the Chinese who were awaiting permission to land, but was to be taken instead to the "Jesus House," as she called the Rescue Home for Chinese slave girls, her anger knew no bounds. She was forced, however, to submit, as the officers had ways and means of accomplishing submission.

Reaching the Home she felt very much out of place in this atmosphere of purity and peace, and had to be watched constantly to see that she did no harm. It was bitterness, indeed, to this evil one to see the many happy faces of the Chinese girls around her, safe in the harbor of home, and to think of the excellent prices they would bring if only—she could sell them.

Instead of that, they would be educated and taught all the domestic arts and womanly virtues, and finally married to Christian Chinese men—men who did not believe in the buying and selling of slaves. O, it was too much!

When she found that she would have to remain in the "Jesus House" until the courts had decided whether or not she could keep the baby, she flew into a rage dreadful to witness. Before any one could realize what she was doing, she dashed at poor little Yute Ho Jai, knocked her down, and gave her several kicks.

Lo Yuen, a tender-hearted girl, rushed quickly to the baby's rescue, and the old hag growled:

"Tell your teacher to let me go out quick!

I do n't want the child. She has brought me too much trouble."

After some days the *ah mo* was set free, but Yutc Ho Jai was kept as a dear little captive, and thus had the distinction of being the youngest prisoner in the United States. To the child that meant happiness and peace, and everything desirable.

And Lo Yuen, the girl who had saved the tot from the old woman's violence, asked the American lady, who was "Mama" to all the Mission girls, if she might be the child's teacher and nurse.

Lo Yuen was blind, as a result of the terrible life she had led when a slave, and, remembering the things from which she had been saved, she desired to give her sweet young life to the cause.

Thus it was that the "Little moon blossom" came into the Home, and unfolded its petals in the sunlight of love.

CHAPTER THREE

IN THE HOUSE OF THE TIGER

WHILE the girl had been telling this story the little moon blossom had fallen asleep with her head in Ah Ching's lap. The newly-found one was filled with a protecting love for the child, and a great yearning to help all the slave girls in existence. She must help—but how? The question was not to be answered to-night, surely, as it was getting late, and Ah Ching realized that she was very tired and sleepy.

"Mama" now came to her and with a protecting arm around the strange child, said:

"Now we are all going to bed, my dear. You will sleep in a room with other girls, so you will not be lonely. I am very glad to see

The Tiger and part of her brood.

that you speak English so well. Who knows what may come of it?"

Then the big iron door was securely fastened, the lights were turned out, and Ah Ching was taken into a cheerful room with many beds of snowy whiteness. Everything was sweet and clean, so different from the dark and dingy cellar home where her bed had been only some planks, covered with a piece of matting.

The kind lady kissed Ah Ching tenderly, and murmured, "Good-night, my child, and God bless you! To-morrow will be the beginning of a new life—a very useful one, I hope, for you."

It was the first time any one had ever kissed her, and she did not understand. But it was pleasant, anyway, and the lady was warm and sweet, and smelled of violets.

Just outside the bedroom was a bath, and into its soothing warmth the tired slave was placed, with minute instructions as to its use. How very clean she felt and looked when she had emerged therefrom, and how heavy her eyelids grew in the delicious warmth of the place.

Next came the bed, so pure and white that the child felt it almost a sin to touch it, much less to slip into its downy purity. How delightful it was! She really intended to lie there and think over all the wonderful happenings of the day.

This was indeed a lovely kind of a tiger, she thought—one that had no claws, and was all love and compassion. If she had claws she certainly did not show them to the poor slaves. Perhaps there was a time and a place for the claws. Who could say?

Then she thought of all that had elapsed since the *ah mo* had fallen into the darkness of the cellar—and then the new highbinder—and the lantern gods.

The other Chinese girls were chattering in subdued undertones, and giggling, as girls, and more especially Chinese girls, will. Surely they were very happy, or they would not be laughing all the time, or be so round and rosy.

"I want to be a part of it all," she reflected—"to be of use in this wonderful place. What can I do?"

Perhaps the Tiger would tell her what to do.

Somehow she felt very glad of the fact that she could speak English. It seemed to give her more confidence in herself, and to put her in touch with the great world with which she had so longed to mingle. She was only a little slave girl, it is true, but now that her prison doors had been opened she felt like a bird set free, and her heart no longer lay like a stone within her breast.

It seemed almost too much happiness to come upon one suddenly. Perhaps she was not big enough to hold it all. There were so many questions in her ignorant heart, but she felt that the Love Lady would answer them all, and she need not worry over them now. Her thoughts soon grew confused, and she could not think connectedly, but when drifting into dreamland she fancied she caught the message:

"Come up—into the light—my dear—little—slave!"

HARE

A Chinese corner in the house of Jessie Juliet Knox.

CHAPTER FOUR

TAI LOY, THE INTERPRETER

WHEN she awoke, the sun was streaming into the room, and some one was bending over her—some one with tawny eyes, and a band of white hair in the brown. She was saying, with the sweetest of smiles, "Good-morning, Ah Ching. Do you feel like getting dressed, and having some breakfast with me?"

Yes, the girl was hungry, and filled with a new life and buoyancy she had never known before. Downstairs she could hear the confused chatter of girlish voices, and frequent squeals.

It did not take her long to array herself in the dainty Chinese garments found on a chair by her bed. Surely some good fairy must have been at work while she slept, for these garments were just the right size, and far more beautiful than those in which she had arrived at the Home.

In a few minutes she, too, was downstairs, answering the greetings of the eager girls who crowded around her.

There seemed to be something unusual going on, and the air was full of excitement.

She had been allowed to sleep later than the others. She enjoyed the food set before her, as only a hungry child could do, and then ventured to ask one of the girls if anything unusual were taking place.

"Yes, our interpreter, Tai Loy, is to be married to-night, and we have to decorate the house and prepare the wedding feast."

Such a remark had a strange sound to the girl, who had never heard of legal marriages and all the festivities attending them. She had not known that a girl ever married a man because she loved him, but had supposed all were slaves, to be bought with gold. She had yet many things to learn, for her life was to be an eventful one, and there were never any dull moments or lack of excitement in the House of the Tiger.

What busy girls they were! In their working clothes of plain black sateen and gingham they hurried here and there, upstairs and down, scrubbing, cleaning, making strings of white roses and evergreen to adorn the rooms, and giving a touch here and another there, until the whole house was transformed into a bower of fragrant loveliness.

"Is the bride crying?" asked Ah Ching, knowing only the heathen custom that a bride-elect must weep violently for three days previous to the wedding, and must stay shut up in her room.

"Why, no! Why should she weep? She is to marry the man she loves, and is very,

very happy. There is nothing to cause tears."

The little bride-to-be was in her room, it is true, but only because she was so busy with her packing. She was to leave immediately after the ceremony for the East, where her future husband was a prosperous merchant.

"O," thought Ah Ching, "If I could only have a peep at a really bride-to-be!" It seemed to her a very wonderful thing, and she longed to see the one who had passed through sorrows, similar, perhaps, to hers, but who was now free from them all.

What had been her story? How strong and capable she must have been to become interpreter, and such a valued assistant to the brave Lady of Love.

To be interpreter, to accompany this fearless one in her rescues—it seemed almost too much joy for one girl to contain. And the thought prompted the question, "Who—who will be interpreter now?" and her heart seemed to stand still as her companion replied, "'*M gee neh*! (I do not know). It is a hard place to fill—a dangerous one, too."

"Of course, a girl is taking her life in her hands when she goes into the haunts of the highbinders, to snatch their prey, and Mama does not know yet what she will do for an interpreter when Tai Loy is gone."

A bold idea forced itself upon Ah Ching's attention, but it was too bright—too daring a thought to entertain.

No, no; it could not be, and yet—the lantern fairies were wonderful beings, perhaps they might even—

Meanwhile, the little bride-elect was tired, and had ceased packing, to indulge in one last girlish reverie. Her thoughts were away over in China—the upside-down-country, where she had been born and knew only a cellar home. She had never known the reality of childhood, the joy of flowers, of sunshine, save the bits to be obtained when she went out to deliver lottery tickets, or sprawled on the steps leading down into the underground home.

Tai Loy had learned English from a friend of her father. He had lived in the United States, and, having taken a fancy to the child, had devoted much time to teaching her; he knew not why, unless it was because she was so bright and brave, and learned so rapidly.

She could remember, now, how she had longed to know more of this strange language, and how it had fascinated her. Perhaps—she had then thought—she might some day get a teacher.

Perhaps—but now her thoughts grew sad, for she remembered that just as she was thinking this she had caught sight of a strange man, with fierce-looking eyes, who was going down the steps into her cellar home.

"A strange man with fierce-looking eyes."

At sight of him she was filled with an awful fear, and the whole world seemed to change, all in a minute.

Black clouds floated ominously across the sky, and took away all the blue—flocks of birds hurried homeward, and to the child looked as if they were being chased by a big "cloud dragon."

In her innocent little heathen heart she had believed that it was all due to the advent of this man.

Who could he be? His was not a face to be trusted, surely. Even the cat arched its back in apprehension.

"I wonder where my brother is?" the child had faltered; "I would like to ask him about this man. Perhaps it is *Di See* (devil king) come to punish me for making faces at the 'kitchen god.'

"Perhaps the big dragon in the sky has told him to come and beat me, for I fear the dragon peeped in at the window and saw me do it. O, what shall I do?

"*Goah! goah!*" (brother! brother!) she had called. "Where are you?"

She had looked up and down the joyless streets, but could not see him. She had not dared enter the house—at least by the front entrance.

The crooked streets did not reveal his whereabouts. She wished then that the streets had been straight, so that she could have seen her brother, but that could not be, of course. They must needs be crooked, to deceive the bad spirits, who have the power to go only in a straight line. In winding streets spirits lose the way and can not find the person for whom they seek.

After what had seemed to her childish mind a very long time, she had discovered her brother coming around the corner.

Just then the strange man came out of the

Tai Loy and her brother.

house. Cold chills chased up and down the girl's spine, and she ran down the street, and was out of sight before he could catch her.

He was smoking a long pipe, and perhaps the opium had dulled his senses. At any rate he did not pursue her, and she wound in and out among the devious byways until she at last entered the rear part of her home through a secret passage, which no one but a celestial could ever have found.

The brother, entering at the front door, wondered why his sister should have run away. He did not fear, and why need she? He was not old enough yet to understand, but she, being a girl, and filled with a sensitive intuition, felt that she had cause for fear. The reason, as yet, she knew not.

The mother, always tender and solicitous, and understanding the language of her child's heart, caressed the young girl as she entered, and noticing the hunted look in her face, said:

"*Mea wah?*" (what is it?); and the child replied: "Tell me, *mo chun* (mama—) I do not know.

"Was it—was it *Di See*? and is he going to kill me?"

"No, no; he is not called *Di See*," faltered the mother, "but," (in a low tone) "it seems to me he must be a friend of the evil one. Say no more, my child. I love you. Do you not know?"

"'*Ngau gee*, (Yes, I know) most honorable blossom lady—I know! Tai Loy *knows*."

Just then the boy had come in, asking, "*Nay yok fon mea*?" (have you eaten rice yet?) and the tearful mother responded, "No —not yet—Come! my golden lilies."

The children were hungry, for the coming of the stranger had delayed the dinner, which with the Chinese is usually eaten at four o'clock. They dared not eat, even now, however, until the small bowls of meat and vegetables had been placed on the "god shelf," and the punks lighted before the idols.

All this took time, but there was no help for it. The gods must first be appeased. If not, who could say what dreadful thing might come upon them?

The children were indeed glad when the worship was over, and they had finished touching their heads to the floor in front of the idols.

The bad man was forgotten while chopsticks clicked merrily on the bowls, and the little almond cakes were crushed between the strong white teeth. Home was good, even if it were only a cellar, for there was always mother, and what could be better?

CHAPTER FIVE

INTO FREEDOM

FROM that day Tai Loy did not seem very well. There was no particular malady, but the child appeared to have something on her mind. She herself could not have put this something into words, but the keen eyes of her mother noted it, and divined the reason.

One day she was told that she could go to her grandmother's. This was always delightful, and for a time the girl brightened and felt almost free from the nameless fear which had so long possessed her. Before starting, however, something happened which took away all her happiness.

Her brother came running to her with radiant face, and eyes aglow with delight.

"*Jo mea see goon*?" (what is the matter?) she asked.

"O, I have a teacher!" he shouted.

"I also will have one," she answered, "and then I can learn to speak the English as well as our friend. Will it not be beautiful?"

She glanced at her mother's face, which was filled with such sadness that it seemed to blast all her hopes at that moment, but she dared not hear the answer now.

Of her father she had seen little of late, but she did not mind. He did not understand as mothers do, anyway, and had always seemed to look down upon her because she was only a girl.

Time passed very pleasantly at her grandmother's, where she frequently saw her brother and also her mother. To meet her brother was more pain than pleasure now, though, for the one great desire of her life had been denied her and her brother had a teacher, while she, being a girl, was not allowed to have one.

"Why should I be denied every wish?" she questioned.

"Because you are a girl, sweet blossom," her grandmother sighed.

"But why is a girl not just as good as a boy?" she interrogated.

"I do not know why," sadly responded the old woman; "I only know that it has always been so with the Chinese, and, I fear, will ever be the same. You must submit to any fate that man sees fit to put upon you, and bear it in silence."

The child felt now, more than ever, the great barrier which had arisen between herself and her brother. She learned to sew and embroider, but what was that? Her mind was vacant, for it had nothing to fill it.

One fateful day her grandfather sent for her. When she entered his room whom should she see but—the man with the fierce-looking eyes? She started and turned pale, and in that moment realized that the gods were powerless to help her, and that this man, whoever he might be, was stronger than all the gods. She could not have uttered a word had her life depended upon it.

Meanwhile the stranger tapped her on the head, examined her body, and seemed to be looking right through her.

The grandfather was saying, "Pretty girl, good girl" in a parrot-like way. It was the first time he had ever praised her. Why should he do so now?

The grandmother had always been kind and loving, but the heart of the old man was hard, and his cars dulled to every sound save the clink of gold.

The stranger, however, did not seem to agree with the old man, for he responded with merely an ominous shake of the head, and, as if he were speaking of a chicken, said, "No good—too thin—too little."

Tai Loy wondered what it could matter to a stranger how thin or how little she might be.

When she was released she ran to her mother, who happened to be there at the time.

"O mother!" she sobbed, clinging to her with nervous fingers; "Has *Di See* come to take me? Will he kill me, do you think?"

But the mother could not reply, for all was mystery as yet, and she knew nothing, except that the old man hated girls and loved money. With her knowledge of Chinese ways, however, she gently said:

"I know your grandfather's rice crop has failed for two years. Perhaps—he is going to sell you to the man."

In despair the girl crept again to the old man's door, creeping in cautiously. She saw the stranger counting out money, while he muttered, "Too muchee, too muchee." Then, alas! she knew that she was being sold.

Running to her mother she fell at her feet in an agony of tears. She knew there was no escape.

The agonized mother could do nothing. Being a poor heathen woman there was nothing for it save to allow her precious child to be torn from her arms, to go into what fate she knew not.

Soon came the parting between mother and child. Tai Loy's heart felt like a stone in her breast.

It was night when the fierce-browed stranger took her away and placed her on a ship, where she found many other Chinese girls, some bought and others stolen, but all huddled together like frightened sheep. None of the girls knew whither they were going. Had they known, they would all have prayed for death.

They could not supplicate the idols, as they had been left behind, and they had never, as yet, even heard of that God who requires neither incense nor bowls of food.

After many bitter weeks they came into port and landed at the docks in San Francisco. The poor, frightened slaves were led down the gangplank and into a crowd of people, strange in feature and costume, then hustled into a gloomy room with other Chinese people. But the fierce stranger remained with them.

Some curious white tickets were produced, and seemed to be very important. After these had been passed upon, the man placed all the girls in a conveyance, and they were whirled roughly along the cobbled streets, and driven like cattle into a gloomy alley of the great Chinatown of San Francisco. Here Tai Loy was separated from her companions.

"A gloomy alley of the great Chinatown."

As there was only one door to her room, and that was always kept locked from the outside, there was no chance of escape, though the poor girl paced the floor, trying to find some means of freedom.

She could not eat; the roses had all gone from her cheeks, and there were great circles around her eyes.

"I am glad!" she cried, "for now I may die."

One day at noon the fierce-looking man opened the door. There was another man with him—Quan Lee—and this man had a kind face, and asked in a pleasant voice: "Is this my girl?"

"Yes," said the bad man, "this is the one."

"And her price?"

"Five hundred dollars."

Quan Lee looked at her and examined her carefully, saying she was "*gowsi*, (pretty) but not very strong looking." The wicked man said, "That is only because she cries all the time."

With the instinct of a child Tai Loy now begged Quan Lee, "O, please buy me, gracious sir! I will be so good!"

This appeal touched the man, who then handed the gold to the master. Taking the girl kindly by the hand he led her into the street and to his own home, where she was cordially welcomed by his wife, whose woman's heart went out at once to the motherless child, while tears of pity came into her eyes.

Life glided on peacefully for a while, until one day Quan Lee's wife fainted.

Tai Loy rushed out to get some one to come to her assistance, and met a young Chinese man who had often come to Quan Lee's house, and who had secretly loved this sweet girl from the first time he met her.

She, in her innocent heart, being really nothing but a child as yet, had a feeling somewhat of reverence for the handsome young Ah Teng, who had always spoken so kindly to her, and treated her with such respect.

As she hurried out he whispered to her and said, "Tai Loy, you are to be sold in a few days to a wealthy man in Sacramento. He will give five thousand dollars for you. Little one, I know the life into which they would sell you, and I can not bear to see this done, and so—I intend to save you. If you will come to the foot of these steps to-night at midnight a friend whom you can trust will be there to take you away."

It chanced that Quan Lee was out of the city that night, and the door was left unlocked.

At the hour appointed the girl slipped into the darkness and the friend was there, closely following her with whispered instructions as they ran. Her heart was almost jumping out of her body, fancying all sorts of horrible things in the gloom, until at last she was bidden to pause, and found herself in a quiet street, outside of Chinatown.

Through the dense fog she could dimly see the form of her guide, who now beckoned her to a gate and whispered, "Tap on the window; there is a 'Jesus woman' inside, and she will be '*pong yow.*'" (A good friend.) And so she was.

In less than an hour she had taken the trembling slave to the Rescue Home.

Who can ever say what peace this brought to the poor captive? To love and be loved; to have friends and teachers, and at last learn to know the great God of Love. Also, to be permitted to see her friend, Ah Teng. Ah, what joy when he, too, as time went on, grew to be a Christian and a great favorite in the Home.

But the best of all, in the list of Tai Loy's blessings was the fact that her own mother had been sent for. She had come from

China, and had lived in the Home all these years, working faithfully, and taking the part of a mother and a helper to these poor motherless ones.

Tai Loy had been such a brave girl, and proved to be so bright and capable that she had been selected as interpreter, and had filled this position for several years.

Many were the heartaches at the thought of giving her up.

And who would take her place?

CHAPTER SIX

THE WEDDING

As TAI LOY thus mused upon her past life a feeling of thanksgiving welled up in her heart, when she remembered the sorrows of the past and how the Tiger had lifted her out of them all and bestowed upon her the boon of freedom. Now she felt that she had no wish ungratified—she was to marry the man she loved, while her dear mother would follow her soon and share her new home.

The only pang was in leaving Miss Cameron and the girls, but she would at times receive visits from them, and could come back and see them occasionally. She had learned all the details of housekeeping in the American way, and had no misgivings on that score. Her little home should be dainty and sweet, not like the heathen homes she had seen in her rescues. . . . But she must no longer sit musing, as time was flying, so, bidding good-bye to her girlish reveries, she arose just as the maids who were to deck the bride came into the room.

These girls all talked to each other in English, but sometimes, in great moments, the Chinese words slipped out, and flowed on until some of the teachers or "Mama" entered the room, when all became at once very proper little ladies, who spoke only the English tongue. It is true they made many mistakes, but they were always such delightful ones that it only added to their charm.

All was excitement now in the big stone building on Sacramento Street, and even from the outside a passer-by might see that something unusual was in progress. The door bell was kept constantly ringing, for there were many packages to be delivered here to-day.

During her years of usefulness at the Mission, Tai Loy had made a wide circle of friends, both American and Chinese, and now they were all glad to send their tribute of love, in the form of dainty gifts, to the dear little Chinese bride.

Each time the door bell rang a crowd of merry girls might have been seen by one who knew where to look, peeping down from the upper floor, giggling and crowding each other in the best of good humor. Chinese girls are more curious than any girls in the world, and surely this was an occasion to call forth curiosity from any one. So many parcels there were, and alluring glimpses of white ribbon tied to tiny cards—O, how perfectly delightful to be a bride, and to receive all those mysterious packages!

The privileged ones followed these bundles

up into the very room for which they were destined—the room of the little bride, who was loved by all the girls, big and little. While the gifts were being opened, all who could do so squeezed into the room, and talked at the same time, and, it is to be feared, forgot to speak English at this critical moment.

Down in the kitchen, too, things were rushing, and the delightful odors which came from that vicinity gave evidence of the fact that Miss Cameron's girls knew how to cook. How proud they were to be allowed to prepare the wedding supper—for they had done everything, with the exception of the bride's cake. This had come from a Chinese friend, and its beauty was not to be revealed before the all-important moment. It reposed in state inside a closet, of which "Mama" carried the key. As it was a wedding cake it should not, properly, be seen until there had been a wedding.

In all the rooms the older girls were dressing the little ones, and woe unto the luckless tot who did not stand quite still while this process of adornment was going on.

Just as the ceremony of dressing the bride's hair was proceeding, the door bell rang loudly, and those who leaned from the railing caught a whiff of fragrance which was surely the most intoxicating perfume ever wafted into their midst.

What could this be?

It seemed to breathe of beauty and love, and its sweet message had already preceded it to the bridal room, even before it was placed in the hands of the one for whom it was intended.

It was a large bouquet of orange blossoms!

Who could have sent it?

Their keen eyes soon discovered a card, which bore a well-known name with a mes-

Ah Teng.

sage; but the name meant little to them, as the giver would always be called by the girls—"the Jesus woman."

Although the girls were to be garbed in Chinese clothes, the bride must, upon this occasion, don American garments, as she was now to step out from the shelter of this haven of peace and take her place in the big world, where she would mingle with American people. She must conform to their customs, and do as they did, in all ways that were good.

So, when at last all the finishing touches had been given, and the wedding march was being played by one of the girls, a modest celestial maiden, transformed into a stylishly-gowned American girl, walked into the rose-embowered room leaning upon the arm of the groom, who chanced to be none other than our old friend—Ah Teng—the young man who had long ago planned her escape.

This was his reward for the noble act—

to have and to hold, as a priceless jewel, the sweet girl whom he had rescued.

And who was this small, ivory-tinted fairy, bearing a golden wedding ring upon a white satin cushion, who felt as if the responsibility of the whole occasion rested upon her tiny shoulders? Why—our "good little moon," to be sure, for who could fulfill this office more gracefully than she—the baby of the Home?

"It is all so wonderful," murmured Ah Ching, the newly-rescued one.

"I did not dream anything could be so lovely," and her heart gave a great throb of joy upon remembering that she now belonged to this big happy family.

Another lovely vision, garbed in the delicately-tinted robes of the Orient, with jeweled hair done in a coil over one ear, now advanced in front of the bridal couple, carrying a golden basket of roses, strewing them for the feet of the happy pair to tread upon. This was a pleasant task, and one that seemed quite fitting for Soy Seen, who herself was just like a fragrant blossom, and was called "Tea Rose," or the "Beauty of the Mission."

It was a very difficult part which "The Tiger" had to take—that of "giving the bride away," and she had to use all her wonderful self-control now to keep from thinking over the sweetness of her acquaintance with the timid little bride. She dared not allow her thoughts to dwell upon the thrilling rescues they had made together, or of how bravely the girl had risked her life, thinking never of herself, but only of the safety of her foster-mother.

And then the heart-to-heart talks they would have afterward, and the secrets which had been poured into Mama's ears when it was found that the brave young Ah Teng had set his true heart upon the girl.

The real Chinese Mama, and Mama Cameron had admitted to Tai Loy that it was indeed a very wonderful thing—and that, of course, there had never been anything quite so sweet and so wonderful before.

But such things were not to be thought of now. O no! and Miss Cameron had to blink and blink, and swallow a big lump which would persist in coming up into her throat, for it would never do to have such a rude thing as a tear trickle down upon the silken folds of her new gown, made for this very occasion.

The Chinese Mama did not cry, of course, for Chinese Mamas are too wise for such foolish things as tears. She only sat with tightly clasped hands, shutting her mind to the past, and dreaming dreams of the future, which must be a rosy one, for—were not all things possible to The Tiger?

When the short ceremony was over, and the girl, who was now no longer the Interpreter, but Mrs. Teng, or *Ah Teng Som*,

The wedding cake!

had been duly congratulated, her husband receiving his share of the ovation, the crowd repaired to the dining room. Here the beauty of things almost took away their breath.

Tai Loy's eyes filled with tears as she now realized for the first time how much the dear girls must really have loved her to have done all this, for surely nothing but love could have transformed an ordinary room into such a fairy bower.

The long table in snowy linen bore just the dainties that Chinese girls love. The mysterious cupboard had been unlocked, for there, occupying the place of honor in the center of the table, was—the wedding cake!

Some of the girls, wearing white Chinese aprons, served in their matchless way, and great was the merriment provoked by the toasts, and many were the healths quaffed in tiny bowls of delicious tea. If there were any sorrow in life, it was all forgotten now, and

Ah Ching laughed and drank tea with the rest, and stabbed the amber of the preserved ginger with the diminutive silver forks, nibbling watermelon seed, and wondering why she could ever have thought life sad.

When her turn came, she drank the small bowl of tea, and gave a toast—first, to "the lantern fairies," and then to the bride and groom.

As she did this, the great lantern of teakwood, which hung directly over the table, seemed to give a start of pleased surprise to know that Ah Ching remembered.

When the feast was ended, good-byes must be said. The carriage rattled down the cobbled streets, while in true American style, which is, after all, Chinese in origin, the happy pair were pelted with rice, and old sandals thrown after them.

When the train sped away, bearing the couple to their new home in the East, the last thing they saw was the tender face of Mama Cameron, smiling and throwing kisses, and murmuring, "God bless you!"

They did not know, nor did any one, that when at last the tired Lady of Love retired into the sanctity of her room that night, the smiles all went away—and her pillow was wet with tears.

CHAPTER SEVEN

A LITTLE MAID OF MONTEREY

After the excitement of the wedding was over, and the household had regained its usual dignity and order, Ah Ching began to realize what a wonderful thing it was to live in this big place, with nothing but happy people around her.

She was placed at once in the school room with the other girls, where she found that speaking English was vastly different from learning to read it, by those queer looking little black things on the page. They were so unlike the big, picturesque characters of her own language. Chinese young people, however, make excellent students, and as Ah Ching loved to learn anything useful, she soon made great progress.

The time for Miss Cameron's vacation was drawing near, and, although her girls always felt sad when they had to give her up, yet they were also very glad for her. She, of all people, needed a rest, and no one knew this better than they. She usually took one of the girls with her on these trips, and of course there was a great deal of conjecture as to who would be the lucky one this time.

One morning while Ah Ching assisted in washing the breakfast dishes, she was thinking about this, and saying to herself, "What happiness it must be to go with Mama on her vacation. I suppose she takes only the girls who have been here a long time. I wonder if—"

Just at this point in her reflections Mama entered the room, where the merry girls were at work, and said:

"Come into the chapel a moment, girls! I want to ask you all a question."

Dropping their work, they stepped into the chapel where the others were, and Miss Cameron said:

"Now, my dears, the time has come again for my vacation, and, as you know, I can take only one girl with me. I love you all dearly, and would like to take every one of you, but as that can not be, I have had to decide upon one, and I wish to know if you all agree with me."

"If you do, I would like to take my very newest daughter—Ah Ching. What do you say, girls?"

"*Hola! Hola!*" (Yes, good, good) came in a deafening chorus, some speaking in Chinese, and some in English.

For a moment Ah Ching sat dazed, so full of joy that she could not speak. An American girl might have thrown her arms around Miss Cameron, and thanked her with kisses, but this timid Chinese girl had not associated with

American people long enough to acquire their freedom, and so only turned red and blinked back the tears, while she stammered: "O, I can never thank you enough, dear Mama!"

The one, however, who loved all these Chinese girls had the faculty of understanding the things they did not say as well as the things they did say.

Meanwhile the heart of the newly-rescued one kept chanting the refrain: "I am going to Monterey with Mama! I shall go in a boat and dance over the blue waves. I am going, I am going."

In historic old Monterey it is beautiful in all seasons, but Ah Ching did not see how anything in the world could be fairer than Monterey in summer, as they stepped from the train and looked upon the broad expanse of the blue bay, whose surface was dotted with hundreds of boats.

Although she had heard that there was a

Chinatown in old Monterey, and a Chinese fishing hamlet in New Monterey, she did not wish to visit either, for fear she might see some one who had known her in the old life.

The days flew by as if on wings, with long, delightful walks through the pines, sails on the blue bay, fishing, bathing, and all the seaside delights which unfolded a new world to this maiden.

. . . And all the while in the fishing hamlet of old Monterey another little slave was longing for freedom—but The Tiger did not know.

All the fishing boats were anchored, for the fish had been brought in early in the day, and the men were resting until the night should come, when they would take their lights and go out fishing for "squid." The torches would transform the darkness of the scene into a perfect fairy land.

Then it was that Choy Ying, the unhappy

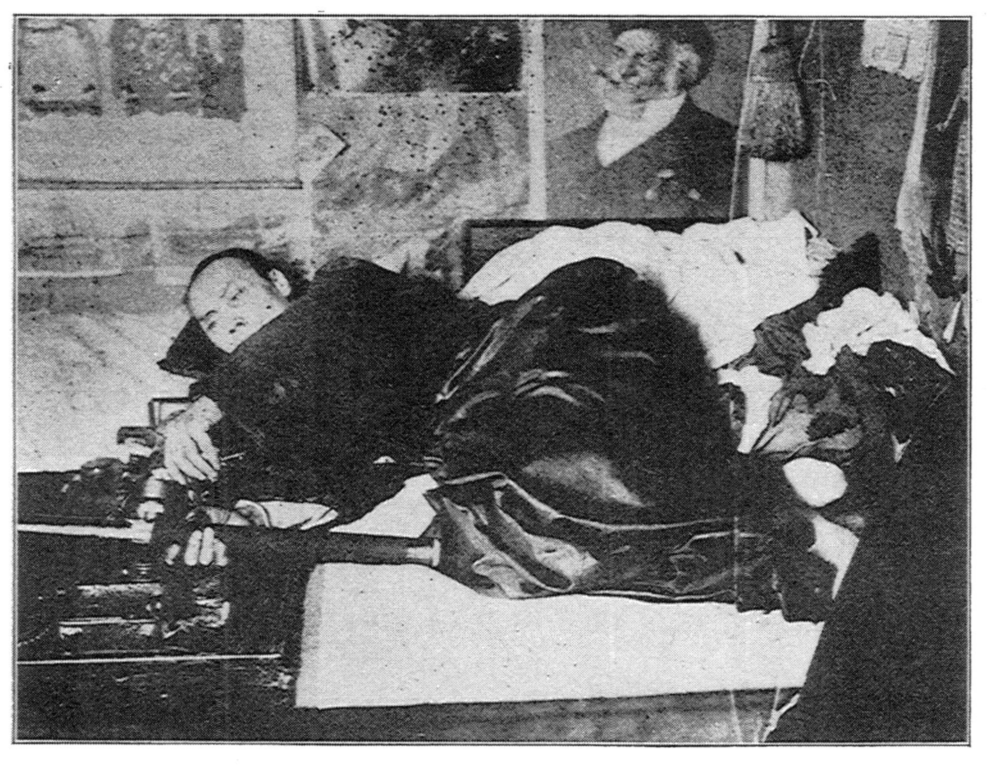

"And her master had fallen asleep over his opium pipe."

slave girl in the old fishing hamlet, was standing inside the back door of one of the patchwork huts of the picturesque but dirty place, gazing at the twinkling lights, longing to be free.

Sometimes when she lay awake at night, listening to the boom of the sullen waves upon the rocks which surrounded her rude abode, she was almost tempted to slip out and throw herself into the angry water, for then she would not have to work so hard and to eat her heart out with longing for something better.

The place she called home was an interesting spot to an outsider, but the child was kept so busy baiting the big hooks and nets, beside doing the housework in the rickety hut, that she had no time to study the interesting part of it. The only leisure she had was when the boats had come in, and her master had fallen asleep over his opium pipe. From this slumber it was the duty of the slave to awaken him in time for the squid fishing at night. She breathed a sigh of relief when she saw that he was asleep, and she might rest a little.

On either side of this village, on stilts, was a small beach, where the sand was like snow, and the little coves sheltered by great rocks. At this place the water near the shore was clear, and here the Chinese girls loved to go barefoot and gather dainty "rice shells," and all the rare sea beauties which young eyes can discover.

To one of these beaches the girl now strayed, amusing herself for a while, and busying her brain with bright images of what might be if she were not a slave.

She discovered two baby star-fish, just alike, and, O, so tiny.

"I think they must be twins," she mused, and wrapping them carefully in her handkerchief she placed them in the square pocket

"The village on stilts."

always inside a Chinese blouse. Stepping into a boat that lay upon the sands she mused upon the subject of the mysterious and many-mooded ocean.

Something lovely had once come into her life—a something she would never forget. She had been allowed to go for a sail with her master in the "glass-bottomed boat," and had gazed with rapture and astonishment upon the wonderful gardens at the bottom of the sea. She thought of this now, as she crouched down in the boat, warmed by the sun and fanned by the sea breeze.

"I am so tired; I guess I will rest here a little while—for it—will soon—be time to awaken—the—master."

CHAPTER EIGHT

THE SEA GARDENS

How cozy it was in the boat! How—

Why! What could this mean?

Perched on the end of the boat was a small fairy, dressed in Chinese robes of green silk. Her hair looked like brown seaweed, and there were frills, like sea foam, on the edges of her garments. She was covered with jewels, which all Chinese girls love. Her necklace was of tiny shells, her sandals of pearls, and for rosettes were two small star-fish—just like the ones Choy Ying had in her pocket.

The tiny fairy now addressed her in a very aristocratic and squeaky voice, and the message, being translated, was:

To the gardens of the sea, come let us flee!
And a birthday dinner you shall see.

"To the gardens of the sea?" gasped the frightened child. "Do you mean to the bottom of the big ocean?"

"*Hilo!*" (Yes) squeaked the fairy, "but do not be afraid, *Ah mooie* (little sister), for I will take good care of you."

"I can not go in this old *sohm* (blouse) and these old *foo* (trousers), can I?" continued the girl.

"*Hilo!*" responded the fairy, "for I will give you fine new garments when we reach the bottom of the sea."

So saying, she fastened two dear little gauze wings on the shoulders of Choy Ying, who felt herself flying through the air, until they were just opposite the Del Monte Hotel.

Before she could say anything about being afraid, she found herself down under the waves, and was surprised to discover that she could see quite as well under water as she could on land, and that it did not make her a bit wet, but was all soft and velvety.

And now they walked through the choicest gardens—far lovelier than those in the Del Monte grounds.

"O, please let me stop and gather some of the pretty things," she pleaded; but the fairy said kindly:

"No, *samen jai*, we must hasten onward to the birthday dinner of—the Star-Fish Twins!"

The Star-Fish Twins! Could those have been the Star-Fish Twins that she found? She felt in her pocket, and—they were gone!

"These are the children of the Prince and Princess Star-Fish," announced the fairy. "I have told them to expect a little earth-maiden, and you, my dear *mooie-jai*, are to be the honored one."

And even as she spoke the faint sound of music floated out through the water. It did

"A little earth-maiden."

not sound at all like the harsh heathen music to which the child's ears were accustomed, but was far too delicate to describe. As they advanced, it grew more distinct, and, when at last they had entered the palace of the Prince, it swelled into a perfect flood of melody.

They were greeted by two star-fish, no bigger than a piece of Chinese "copper cash." They had voices as wee as themselves, and talked in the best Cantonese dialect. Choy Ying had never even dreamed that fish could talk, to say nothing of being able to converse in Chinese; but then, how coarse and ignorant are the people who live on land compared with the fairies of sea and sky.

The small pages now conducted her to the royal presence, where she was welcomed by the Prince and Princess, who gave their fingers, one at a time, until each had been shaken. It was rather tedious, but, of course, all the proprieties must be observed.

The palace was down between two huge boulders, which were completely covered with pearl. A page touched a hidden spring, and the whole place was flooded with light that glowed and shimmered on the pearl, until the girl's eyes were fairly dazzled, and she saw, quite distinctly, the assembled guests and gorgeous furnishings of this rare palace under the sea. There were soft carpets of green moss, and carpets of velvet. Great bushes of rose and lavender coral grew here and there, while tall trees of feathery amber swayed in the waves, their branches filled with the babies of all the Fish families.

After a time spent in conversation—the tiniest, squeakiest conversation Choy Ying had ever heard, a fairy announced that dinner was served—the birthday dinner of the royal twins!

Choy Ying at once thought of her shabby garments, but, on looking down, was greatly surprised to see no shabby garments at all, but, instead, a dazzling robe of green and silver gauze.

She was conducted to the place of honor at the table. What a curious company was gathered there!

First, there were the Prince and Princess Star-Fish, who were very large, and of a bright red color, each having as many as twenty fingers.

In Fish Land no one but royalty ever had so many points. There were also the Star-Fish children, a long row of them. Some were little and some were big, and they were all colors of the rainbow. Next the Princess sat the royal twins, no bigger than Choy Ying's nail; and be it known that they did not cry or tease at the table, and were perfectly satisfied with everything to which they were served.

Then came the Abalone family, saying that

they had had quite a time getting away from home, as they were all fastened so tightly to a rock that they almost tore their pretty gowns getting loose. Still, they did get loose, and were here enjoying themselves to the utmost, repeating in parrot-like voices, "All's well that ends well."

Next appeared the Sea Urchins. O my! how funny they did look—a great row of them, all covered with stickers. They wore gowns of red and purple and brown, and Choy Ying remembered seeing whole families of them when she was out in the glass-bottomed boat. The master had called them "Chrysanthemum Beds." "Chrysanthemum Beds," indeed! Did not that prove how little the land folk knew?

Some of this family happened to remember her, too, for they had been much interested in the pretty face staring down at them so intently through the glass bottom of the boat.

O, they had good memories, had the Sea Urchins! They were indeed beautiful to look upon, yet she distinctly heard Madam Jelly Fish whisper to the Princess and say, "I would rather not sit with the Sea Urchins, if it please Your Highness, because they have a habit of jabbing one in the side with their stickers."

Unfortunately, these same Sea Urchins were great on shaking hands, and when Choy Ying came to them their stickers punched into her hands, so that she was glad when the end of the row had been reached. However, they meant well, she was sure, and were really a very jolly family.

The purple and lavender babies of this family got to giggling at the table, much the same as land babies do, but one look from the big, bristly papa, and one shake from his hundred fingers, made them stop giggling and look as sober and demure as it is possible for a Sea Urchin to look.

Papa and Mama Jelly Fish looked funnier than any one there, thought the girl, for they were so fat and wobbly and you could see right through them. She could not see how they ate or where they put their food, but they surely must eat something or they would not be so fat and wobbly and good natured. They could hardly keep their places at the table, though, because they were so slippery, and some of the Jelly Fish children were all the time sliding off their chairs and under the table, having to be picked up in a dust pan by the sea fairies.

Then there were the Sea Anemones, which at first Choy Ying had taken for pretty green and white sunflowers. Sitting still they looked like sunflowers, but when any one touched them they would draw up in a knot.

Choy Ying ventured to shake hands with Mrs. Sea Anemone, but had cause to regret it when this lady took the girl's finger in her mouth and pinched it, until she thought she would never see it again. She just had to stand there until the sunflower lady drew a long breath, when—out dropped the finger. From that moment she was careful not to shake hands with any more of the Anemone family. They were very nice to look at, but one really could n't afford to be on friendly terms with such people.

The Jelly Fish infants kept laughing at the Crab children, because they looked so funny walking sidewise on their claws. Baby Crab then gave baby Jelly Fish a nudge in the side, and that stopped the giggling.

There were, of course, many other families at this feast, among whom were the Flounders, who never looked where they sat, but always flopped down upon some of the guests.

The Salmon were very haughty and stuck-up because of their popularity with human beings. The Devil Fish laughed in his horns as he thought of this, for he could not see what the Salmon gained by it.

When all were at last seated, the feast began, while strains of rare music floated from the Fish Orchestra, which was artfully concealed in one of the huge kelp trees.

Choy Ying here ventured to remark that the music was *gowsi* (pretty), but her voice sounded so big that it frightened the baby fish in the tree nursery, and they all began crying for their mamas. Then there was a queer, wriggling sound of all the mamas darting from the table to comfort their babies, and explain to them, with many fishy endearments, that this girl lived upon the land where it was the custom to talk in that big way, but that she was really a very good little girl, after all, and would not harm them.

. . . Just at this point a very loud, shrill whistle was heard. It startled Choy

Ying, for it did not seem at all as if it belonged to this beautiful fairy land of the sea. It grew louder and more insistent.

Suddenly the girl looked around her, and —why—the fishes had gone—the palace, too, had gone—and she and her tiny craft were afloat on the bay, with no oars, and nothing but the sky for a covering.

It was late, and—the master had not been awakened.

O, he would surely kill her for this.

But what was that stately vessel approaching her small craft? It was a steamer, and leaning over its side was—none other than our dear Ah Ching, who, although she knew it not, was about to make her first rescue.

As the big vessel stopped, Ah Ching, before any one could take note of what she did, slipped down the steps which had been lowered, and reaching out both hands to the dazed *mooie jai* in the rocking boat, said,

"You shall come to live with my dear Tiger Lady. Do not fear!"

When the bewildered child had reached the deck, she found there this wonderful person, who kissed away her fears, and promised that the master should never again have possession of her.

How fortunate that Miss Cameron had decided to make the return trip by water!

And the happy child said to herself, as they passed through the Golden Gate:

"I know—I know—it was the Sea Fairy."

CHAPTER NINE

THE GIRL FROM CHINA

WHEN the three tired but happy wanderers reached San Francisco it was dark, and the lights of the great city were twinkling cheerily, as if in welcome to the shabby little stranger within its gates.

Ah Ching was indeed acting the part of interpreter now, and it made the girl's heart thrill to think she was being of some use to Mama.

In her heart she had one great desire, but dared not give utterance to it.

The girls at the Home were not greatly surprised when they discovered the little stranger, as it was no uncommon event for a girl to arrive at any time, and under any circumstance. They welcomed her, and she could hardly believe it true that she was really to live in this bright, cheerful place. Already it seemed like a dream—the dirty fisherman's hut, the hard work and loveless existence, with no company but the sullen waves booming on the rocks.

"I am going to forget it all," she said aloud, "and will only remember that I am in my own home, with lots of sisters and the dearest Mama in the world."

Miss Cameron was greatly touched at this, for she, of all people, knew what it must have cost a timid Chinese girl to say so much.

Awaiting them was a nice hot supper, and as the others had all finished their evening meal, the two girls ate with Mama in her private dining room. To make them feel more at home she also ate with chop sticks and drank her tea from Chinese bowls. They had such a merry time that it took away all the feeling of strangeness which might have been present.

The tired *mooie jai*—now no longer slave, but a free little soul—was put to bed in a room with several other girls. Ah Ching, also, though very weary, was very happy. Just as she was dozing off she was awakened by the touch of a soft hand, while the voice of her newly-found Mama whispered a wonderful question in her ear—surely the most wonderful question Ah Ching had ever heard. It was—

"Would you like to be my interpreter, and go with me to make my rescues?"

For an instant her heart almost stopped beating. Surely, ah, surely, she must be dreaming. This must be like the fairy vision of the little fisher-maiden. But no! the hand was real, for she could feel the ring—the pretty Chinese one—and, as the moon shone in through the window, she could plainly see the band of white hair aslant the brown. Her wonderful desire had come true. So this was what the lantern fairies had meant when they had so often chanted to her in the old days. This was "coming up into the light." And, best of all, it was now to be her privilege to bring other poor slaves "up into the light."

About a week after this, when the little fisher-maiden had begun to feel quite at home, and Ah Ching had almost forgotten the old life, Miss Cameron received a cablegram from China. A girl who had been attending one of the Mission Schools in Hong Kong had disappeared—no one knew how or where. She had been stolen in the night, and the teachers in the school had reason to believe that Yuen Luey had been taken to San Francisco to be sold as a slave; so this message was for Miss Cameron to watch the landing of the steamers from China, to see whether a girl answering to Yuen Luey's description would arrive.

Ah! now life had really begun for Ah Ching. She could hardly wait until the steamer was due, to begin her duties as interpreter; but at last the day came, and, her heart beating with delight, the child stepped into the closed carriage with Miss Cameron and an officer, and started out over the cobbled streets and down to the dock, to search for the little prisoner.

O, what if she should not come, after all? Surely there were many places besides San Francisco to which they might take her, and the heart of Ah Ching grew cold with fear, until she looked into the calm and hopeful eyes of The Tiger—the Tiger who was getting ready to spring.

At last the steamer came into view. Ah Ching was all eyes now, and as the great vessel neared the docks she happened to be the very first person to see crouching behind a sinister-looking Chinaman some one—a very white and timid some one. Even before Miss Cameron had time to speak, and as soon as the Chinese passengers had landed, the brave little interpreter, fearing the child might again be spirited away, rushed to the end of the gangplank and grasped her, whispering these words in her ear: "Is this Yuen Luey? O, tell me truly, for we are your friends, and will take you away from the wicked man."

With a glance of fear at the man the child sobbed "*Hilo!*" (yes) and without another word the cruel Chinaman found himself in the hands of the law, while Mama, folding her new daughter in her arms, placed her in the carriage.

"It really made one's heart ache to see her face."

CHAPTER TEN

YUEN LUEY'S STORY

THAT night Ah Ching, and, indeed, the whole big family, listened to the sad story of Yuen Luey.

She was not a beautiful child, and it really made one's heart ache to see her face, because it looked so old and gave evidence of so much suffering.

"My troubles have all come from ten little yellow prisoners—my ten toes; for, alas! I was an aristocrat, and as you know, it would have been an everlasting disgrace upon my family name if I had been allowed to grow up with feet of the ordinary size. A high-caste girl with big feet? Never! and so my mother had my tender feet bound with stout strips of cloth, turning the toes under, and fastening them back that way.

"I could not, of course, run about in the sunshine or play as other children did, so I grew up pale and delicate.

"If any one asked my mother why she did this she would reply, 'Because every one else does, and so we must.'"

Yuen Luey now paused to hear the sympathetic remarks of others who had been little-footed when they came into the Home, but who now had their feet unbound.

"My father often used to say," she resumed, "'Some day we will go to San Francisco, in the United States. That is the place where they find gold in the streets.' He had plenty of money, but never seemed satisfied.

"'I should not care if I did find gold in the streets,' I used to say, because I knew the gold could not take the pain from my feet, unless—I could have them unbound. But no! I could not do that, for then I should no longer be an aristocrat.

"Did it hurt, do you think, to have my toes doubled under and wrapped so tightly? O yes! no one will ever know how badly, and how my feet ached and burned so that I could not sleep at night, but kept poking my poor, feverish feet out from the covers, trying to find a cool place which might ease the pain.

"'Mother,' I cried one day, when I felt that I could endure it no longer. 'Why do I have to suffer so? What is it all for?' And my mother replied, 'You will forget the pain by and by, when you have a lovely small foot, and a nice rich mother-in-law.'

"The idea of a 'nice, rich mother-in-law' did not appeal to me, for I would so much rather have had nice big feet, and have romped and played with the children of the lower classes.

"How I envied those children as they ran

past my home, but I could only look down from my lofty balcony and long and long for freedom. I knew of no help, though, save that which was supposed to come from the idols, but away back in my heart I did not believe they could help me.

"One day as I leaned over the railing I said to myself, 'I do not believe the goddess *Kwan Yum* cares for children, for I have always prayed to her, and have given her the best of everything. I have begged her many times to have my feet unbound, but she never heeds my prayers. I wonder—if there is any other God.'

"Just then I saw something which made me stop talking to myself. Two American ladies were walking right beneath my balcony. Their costumes seemed very strange to me, but the thing which most impressed me was the fact that they had big feet. O, so big, they seemed. No wonder they wore such long skirts. It was done, of course, to hide their feet. At that time I did not dream that they had no wish to hide their feet, and were not at all ashamed of their size.

"Meanwhile, all the Chinese people were staring at these big-footed white ladies. I was so busily engaged in looking at them that I dropped a piece of embroidery from my fingers, and it fell right down on the heads of the strange ladies, and fluttered in a crumpled little heap on the street.

"They looked up and saw me, and I discovered that they were accompanied by a Chinese interpreter."

"O yes, it was Soy Leen; one of our girls," interrupted Miss Cameron.

"Yes—Soy Leen was her name," replied the girl. "'Can we come up?' this interpreter now asked.

"I dared not give permission without my mother's consent. I longed, however, to know these people, so I called to my mother, and she stepped out and looked down upon the street.

"While the interpreter was explaining to her, my heart almost jumped out of my body with fear that she would refuse, but she did not. From some cause—it may have been only curiosity—she gave her consent.

"This was a wonderful thing, as high caste families are quite unapproachable, and, as you all know, their girls are so jealously guarded that they might almost as well be packed in cotton.

"The ladies, who were missionaries, and trying to gain access to as many homes as possible, were gratified at my mother's consent, and eagerly hastened up the stairway which led to our apartments.

"I had always been considered unlucky, as I was born on the first day of the first month. Just to be a girl was bad enough, without that. But now, as I saw these ladies enter, and read love and understanding in their faces, it seemed to me that at last I was lucky, and that, perhaps—perhaps—these people might even know of some other God. If I had an opportunity, I would inquire, but I did not wish mother to hear.

"The ladies looked sad, as they glanced at my poor, bound feet.

"I listened eagerly to the interpreter as she chatted away, explaining the work of these ladies, and—what was that she was saying? 'The American God always answers prayer?' Ah! now I, a little prisoner to custom, was all attention. My cheeks grew hot and my heart beat rapidly, as I drank in her precious words. I watched my chance, and when mother had stepped into the next room to prepare hot tea for the guests, I eagerly questioned the interpreter, and explained to her: 'Always I have prayed to the goddess *Kwan Yum*,' (and I pointed to the porcelain goddess in her small temple of teakwood, which held a prominent position on our 'god-shelf'). 'Always I have begged one thing of her, but—she does not hear. Can it be—that this new God you speak of would hear me?' I whispered.

"'*Nung!*' (it can) hurriedly returned the girl. 'He always hears, and gives you the desire of your heart, if it is a good one.'

"So I said to her, 'I must tell you what it is. Perhaps you can tell me if it is right. It is—that I may have my feet unbound. You do not know how they hurt all day and all night. *Kwan Yum* does not care, you see, for she has never listened. Do you really think your God would care?'

"The eyes of the ladies were full of tears as they replied, 'Yes, dear, He always cares when the innocent suffer. We will tell Him, and in your heart always ask Him to set you free.'

"Just as I finished," resumed Yuen Luey, "my mother entered the room, carrying tea and cakes, and when all had been served, Soy Leen interpreted thus:

"'We are going to establish a boarding school for girls. There are so many bright girls in Canton that it is a pity they should go without an education.'

"They explained it all to my mother, who, true to her Chinese training, replied:

"'But why should we educate a daughter and spend money on her, only to have her marry, and go into another family? All our money would be wasted.'

"The ladies then endeavored to bring my mother to their way of thinking, explaining it all, and trying to convince her, until finally she faltered, 'Maybe I will let Yuen Luey go. I think so—maybe—How soon?' And then the interpreter said, 'No girls with bound feet can come. It is the rule of the school; but—

we can have Yuen Luey's feet unbound, and then she can come. We had better have it done right away, though, before it becomes more difficult. . . . Do you not know that the Empress has forbidden any more foot binding? You will really be quite out of the style if you leave them bound.'

"With this remark they took their leave, and left my mother to think it over, and to confer with my father on the subject.

"Through my mother's poor, bewildered brain floated terrible visions of 'no mother-in-law, and big feet.'

"Could it be true, I thought, what the ladies had said? That night when I went to bed I clasped my hands, and whispered in the darkness, 'O, nice God! please let me unbind my feet!' After I had said this, a horrible fear came over me. What if—well, I would ask the ladies next time they came.

"They did come again in a few days, after

mother had had ample time to think the matter over; and as soon as they entered the room I whispered to the interpreter while the ladies were being seated, 'Can God speak Chinese?'

"She smiled as she replied, '*Kooie nung, samen jai*, (Yes, child, He can). Our God can speak all languages and understand all hearts.' Then I felt as if a great load had been taken from my mind, and I now listened eagerly to the conversation.

"My mother began by saying, 'The big feet will be very ugly, and there will be no rich mother-in-law.' To this the ladies responded, 'But, to be without pain, and as nature intended, will be better than a dozen mothers-in-law; and besides, the young men will soon find out that little feet are no more *hai tong*, (stylish) and will not care to marry a bound-footed girl.'

"This last argument was too much for

mother, and I could see she was weakening. Child though I was, I could tell that. And all the time a little bird seemed to be singing in my lonely heart, because—the new God could speak Chinese.

"'We are going to make some beautiful silk shoes, all embroidered,' resumed the ladies, 'and they will be for the girls to wear on Sundays. Really, you have no idea how pretty the big feet are when you get used to them, and how nice they will look in those embroidered shoes.'

"Finally my mother gave her consent, and it seemed to me at that moment as if my heart would burst for joy, and I felt that I could even forgive Kwan Yum.

"The ladies did have a lot of shoes made, but they were not the little-footed ones. They took me and soaked my feet in hot water, and unbound the poor, cramped prisoners, until soon they ran around in perfect freedom.

"The school was opened by giving a big dinner. Some one suggested singing a hymn about the unbinding of feet. As there were no such hymns to be found, one of the ladies composed one, and they sang it. Then they talked about foot-binding and how it hurt little girls; how it made them lazy and sick and cross, but how, that when the feet were unbound, the girls would be strong and healthy and have lovely natures. They could walk, instead of having always to ride, and if they were poor they could work and make money. They knew that when the Chinese people learned that refinement and sweet, gentle manners accompanied the big feet they would forget that they ever had a prejudice against them. The interpreter finished by saying:

"'Does not our own Empress have big feet? Are not the shoes of our Empress good enough for us?'

"Next day all the little-footed girls came

to school and asked to have their feet unbound.

"Shortly after this, I was sleeping soundly one night, when I was suddenly awakened by a draught of cold air blowing in upon me. I started to cry out, when a muffler was placed over my mouth. A cloth that had a faint, sweetish odor was pressed against my nose, and I knew no more until I found myself on a big steamer.

"I cried and begged for my parents, but all to no purpose. I knew not where I was going. All was perfect darkness to me, until I stepped from the steamer and into the arms of—"

"The Tiger!" smiled Mama, with a tender embrace, while all the girls came up to speak a good-night word of love to the tired stranger.

That very night Miss Cameron sent a message to the distracted parents, notifying them of the safety of their child.

They at once decided to come to San Francisco, and here, although the father did not find gold in the streets, he did find something much better, and Yuen Luey was permitted to continue her education in the Home, and to know the God who could speak Chinese.

CHAPTER ELEVEN

THE FEAST OF QUAN FOO CHI

It was the Feast of Quan Foo Chi, or, in other words, the Chinese Fourth of July, but the girls in the Home did not celebrate it, because it was a heathen festival, and they had done with such things.

All over California the Chinese people were observing this festive occasion, though, and the girls loved to lean from the windows of the Mission and watch the gayly dressed people of their own nation go by, and catch the squeal of the Chinese fiddles playing in temple and shop. In many ways it was really very much like the American Fourth.

About fifty miles from San Francisco was a beautiful place called San José (San Hozáy),

"Now Ah Nom lived in this Chinatown."

or "The Garden City." It, too, had its Chinatown, in which were many lovely children.

Ah Ching, the new interpreter, had heard so much about the enchanting gardens at this place that she hoped some day to be able to go and see it all for herself, and to visit the Chinese quarters there, and find if there were any little slaves.

Now, Ah Nom lived in this Chinatown, and although she was only six years old, she knew all about the great warrior—Quan Foo Chi, whose birthday they were to celebrate for four long days.

Sometimes, when the child had been supposed to be sleeping, she had overheard her father and mother talking, and knew not whether to be glad or sad at some of the things they said.

They had often conversed about some lady in San Francisco—"*Lo Foo*" (The Tiger) they called her—and told how some of the highbinders hated her, but could not harm her, as she wore an armor. They did not know that it was only the armor of love, but thought she was a witch, or something of that kind.

They told how she was not afraid of anybody, but would grope her way in the darkness at any time, day or night, in the most terrible places, exposing herself to all sorts of danger, and filled with the one desire to save a slave girl at any cost.

Ah Nom's parents were not good to her. All the time, and without any cause, they beat her, also her brother Kee, and the dear baby Lean, who was only two years old.

Ah Nom had heard her father say, "Ping Goy, the highbinder, says he will give me a thousand dollars for Ah Nom, and when the baby is as old we can get a good price for her. I think we had better take it, for we might never again get so good a chance."

The mother had not replied at once, for away back in her heart lurked the germs of mother-love, and, if she had been allowed her choice, she would have kept the child. So this mother-love was pleading and tugging at her heart strings as she replied hesitatingly, "Had we not better wait until she is older?" The father muttered, "Wait? and lose the chance that may never come again? No! we must sell her now, for we need the money."

And she—being only a Chinese woman, and knowing that no words of hers would have any weight with her husband, who was also her master—said no more. He always did as he pleased, anyway, and so, as the trembling child lay upon her hard bunk, she heard her father say:

"We must be very cautious, for if it ever reaches the ears of 'The Tiger' she will stop it, and take the child to live in the 'Jesus House.'"

Ah Nom pondered long upon her father's words. Who could this "Tiger" be? If—she could only find her, but being a girl, she knew of no way of doing so.

And now the father continued, "Have the *samon jai* looking as attractive as possible, for the highbinder will be here on the last day of the festival of Quan Foo Chi."

The child's heart sank within her, for she knew that to-morrow was the first day, and that would mean that she had only four more days before she would fall into the clutches of the unknown. She had long looked forward to this festival, but now there was a weight on her heart, and although she did not feel happy in a home where she was beaten all the time, yet she feared that even a worse fate might overtake her in the hands of the highbinder.

When she awoke, the great dragon flag was flying from the big pole in front of the

Joss House, and the streets were lined with gay lanterns, gorgeous in tint and style. From some of them long silken tassels were hanging, from which were suspended various charms, to keep away evil spirits.

Everything upon which the eye rested was a mass of glowing color. The odor of burning powder and smoking sandal wood filled the air, and the inharmonious banging of tom-toms and the blare of trumpets were as the sweetest music to heathen ears.

Ah Nom, her face thickly covered with rice powder and lips tinted with a vivid patch of carmine, was arrayed in her festive robes.

She had always been a pretty child, and just now her hair was elaborately dressed, and filled with jewels of gold and jade, and she wore a gay pink *sohm* and *foo* of green silk.

There were many rites of worship to be observed, but the children longed to finish with this part of it so that they might run out upon the streets and see the many attractions there.

Ah Nom had never quite understood why her father should call his place a restaurant, when it was not. It was, in reality, a gambling house.

In the front room were rows of large, brown earthenware jars, to make people think this was a little shop, but the jars were always empty, and when an American lady, who was Ah Nom's only friend, had inquired as to their contents, Ah Nom's mother had replied, "Just now all gone. Pletty soon go San Flancisco—buy too muchee."

But they never did.

These things were hard for a child to understand, and the lady friend had told her not to puzzle her little brain over it.

Ah Nom had finished worshiping the idols now, and had stepped out into the street to play with the five children of Ken Toy, the aristocrat who lived next door. How she longed always to play with Leen Soy, who lived across the street, but as this dear little tot's mother had died of a terrible skin disease the father had forbidden Ah Nom to associate with Leen Soy, although the child had no sign of any disease, but was like a dear little blossom. The father had beaten Ah Nom every time she had played with this child, so she dared not repeat the offense.

The American Lady was well known to the "look-out man," who always sat on a stool outside the gambling house door, and who, if he saw the police coming, would press a button to warn the gamblers inside. Then things would be changed in the twinkling of an eye, and when the police entered they would find nothing but a few sleepy looking Chinamen seated at a table smoking long pipes.

But he never pressed the button when this lady came, because all the *tong yon* (Chinese people) knew they had nothing to fear from her. She was just "*pong yow*" (a good friend) to them, and helped them in any way needed.

If they were unjustly persecuted by the "white devils," as so often happened, she took measures to have their wrongs righted.

If they wished to have a tooth pulled or a picture taken she took the timid little Chinese women to the proper place, and brought them safely home again.

She had windows cut in their dark cells, and if they wished to learn to read and write she taught them; if not, she let them alone. She never tried to force her beliefs on them, and worked for love and not for money; and because of this they loved and trusted her. She was very fond of Ah Nom, and every time she came to Chinatown would say to her, "Whose girl are you?" and Ah Nom would throw her thin arms around her neck and be lifted from the ground, while she replied, "I'm *you* gel!"

The friend was much surprised when the child said to her, "You *sábe* (understand) 'Tiger!'"

"Tiger?" said the lady, puzzled at first, but soon a light broke upon her, and she replied:

"The Tiger!—Do you mean Miss Cameron?"

"I no *sabé* Miss Camlon," responded the child; and the friend exclaimed, "Tell me what you mean, Nom! I do know the Tiger, if you mean Miss Cameron, and she is the dearest Tiger in the world. But why do you ask?"

Then Ah Nom drew her around the corner, and whispered words in her ear that made the lady tremble and grow pale, for she dearly loved this little girl, and the things she spoke of seemed too awful to be true.

It does not seem very bad when one just reads of these things, but when one really knows these dear shut-in little maids, and loves them, it cuts the heart like a knife to have them sold as slaves. The lady's heart sank within her, until she remembered—The Tiger!

"Ah Nom, wait! In a few minutes I will come back," she hurriedly whispered.

There was a telephone in a Chinese store on the corner, and on this phone, with closed doors, she was soon talking to—The Tiger! Telephones are wonderful things—almost as wonderful as the little bird that tells things to Miss Cameron.

CHAPTER TWELVE

SOME CHINESE CUSTOMS

EVERY day and night after this the friend came, for she lived near, and wanted to keep guard over the child.

The greatest event of all this great occasion was to be "the burning of the devil," or of "Di See," which was to take place on the fourth night. Di See, the king of all the devils, was represented by a huge paper figure, with hideous features. He was in a tiny house, by the open air theater, and in front of him, on a platform, were kept offerings of food, while red candles and punks burned there day and night.

Ah Nom pulled her friend over to get a good view of him, saying, "I no likee Di See! I allee time scare; him velly ugly."

"Then if you do not like him, why do you kow-tow to him?" inquired the lady.

"Because," replied the child, "if I be good to him then he go back and tell all the bad devils to let me alone for one year."

The lady sighed. Sometimes she almost grew discouraged; it was so hard to battle with superstition and ignorance, but her great love for these child-like people made her always try to help them, although it was such an uphill road.

The hour for the parade drew near, and Ah Nom forgot all her sorrow in the joy of the present moment. The friend, too, enjoyed it all, and clasped tightly the hand of the child, who was jumping up and down with delight.

Soon the procession formed in front of the joss house and started, winding in and out, until it passed through every little street in Chinatown.

The scene was a gay one, for all the happy children in the quarter were arrayed in gorgeous robes, with bright head dresses, some ornamented with tiny mirrors, and all wore richly embroidered trouser-strings and charms.

Long rows of firecrackers hung from the balconies, and a constant fusillade was kept up. All were out to do homage to the parade, or rather, to the Memorial Tablets of Quan Foo Chi, the great and noble one.

These tablets, placed within a carved temple, were held aloft and carried by some of the prominent men.

Such a din was never heard before.

As the temple passed each door, some member of the family would throw out whole packages of "mock money," and as the doors were all so close together, the din was continuous. It would have been of no use to talk, for no one could have heard a word.

The air was stifling with the smoke of fireworks—the band played, and men banged mercilessly on the tom-toms and cymbals, while the shrill sound of the "*de uk jai*" (flute) rose high and insistent above all other sounds.

The most prominent Chinamen were garbed in long silken robes of pale blue and lavender, green and bright pink, and wore gorgeous sashes.

In front was the flag of China, with the dragon, and the embroidered canopies and banners were enough to dazzle one's eyes.

On the third night there was a ceremony called "Chasing the Priests." A crowd of American people sat out on the long balcony of the Chinese restaurant, in order to obtain a good view of this.

Ah Nom was allowed to go with the American friend, and to watch her little face and hear her jolly giggle was of itself entertainment enough. When Ah Nom laughed, everybody laughed. They could not help it, it was so contagious. She leaned far out over the railing, for she did not wish to miss any of it. To her it was a wonderful thing.

Some of the people watched the tea rose face more than they did the performance on the street below. All the time the lady held tightly to the blouse, so that the child could not tumble over.

On the roofs all around could be seen Chinese women, peeping down fearfully. It would have been considered a terrible disgrace for a high caste lady to come out on the street and watch it all. If they did not happen to live where the performance was visible from their roof, then they must go without seeing it; that was all. Many of them had to stay shut away in their apartments, longing and longing for a glimpse of it, and straining their ears to hear the music. To be sure, there was not much difficulty in hearing it, as it could be heard a good many blocks away.

The priests, arrayed in their long robes of red silk with a big embroidered square in the back, had assembled in the street, together with the dear little altar boys, Ah Goon and Ah Won, while the music rose high and shrill above it all.

Five tables were placed in the street, and upon each one was a Memorial Tablet and offerings to the gods. After this the priests knelt in front of each table, on a piece of matting which they carried from place to place. They read the prayers from long crimson books, while the small altar boys who knelt behind them kow-towed in ludicrous imitation of their respected elders.

Then, one at a time the priests began to walk in and out among the tables, followed by the altar boys. More and more quickly they ran, until it turned into a mad chase, while the crowd screamed with laughter, and Ah Nom's hearty giggle could be heard above it all.

Just now she did not remember that she had ever been unhappy, or that she was to be sold as a slave. She only remembered that she was free for a while, and that the two small boys looked very comical as they chased the priests.

The lady put her fingers in her ears, as the long strings of firecrackers were now lighted in the parade. Ah Nom pulled the fingers out again, though, saying, "You listen! Velly pletty; I heap likee."

As they marched to the temple the child tugged at the friend, entreating, "Come, go joss housee! See pliests makem loosteh go sileep!" (See the priests make the rooster go to sleep!)

The lady could not imagine what this meant until they reached the joss house and saw the priest make a rooster stand on the end of a bamboo sword. The Chinese people said that the priests had hypnotized it, but the lady thought perhaps it was only stupefied with opium. This rooster having been raised in the temple was thought worthy to perform before the gods.

At the side of the temple was a long room, where the priests had their meals, and where free dinners were given, on a certain day, to all who cared to partake.

As night came on, the joss house was literally packed with people of all nations, for every one took a great interest in these Chinese festivals.

Ah Nom was much interested, and enjoyed seeing everything around her, but felt a little fear of the gigantic figure of Quan Foo Chi, and that of his brother, who stood towering on either side the door.

"Quan Foo Chi step on dlagon; she bluddeh step on kitty," (Quan Foo Chi is stepping on a dragon; his brother on a kitty) she explained, while the bystanders laughed.

"The gigantic figure of Quan Foo-Chi and his brother."

Yes, the great warrior had his foot resting on a dragon, and that of his brother was placed on a paper tiger (kittie). This represented dominion and power.

The priests were still chanting dolorously from the red books, and the altar boys were getting so sleepy they had to tickle each other's toes to keep awake. They each held a scroll, and two articles, which although they looked like two doll beds, were really memorial tablets, and before these they had to kow-tow every time the priests did.

Goon was so busy gazing at the crowd around him that he just could not remember to kow-tow, until Won would jab him in the side with his fan as a gentle reminder.

Both babies should have been at home in bed, but the Chinese did not think so. They deemed it a great honor. Although the two mamas were shut away back, one in an opium house and the other in rooms which could only be reached with a ladder, and could not see any of it, yet with their own fingers they had fashioned these rich garments for their "honorable sons," and arrayed them proudly therein.

As for the boys, they were very proud and haughty because they had been chosen for such places of honor, and they would scarcely speak to their old friends.

CHAPTER THIRTEEN

DI SEE AND—THE TIGER

It was so beautiful in the joss house, with its gay banners, carved wood, and brass.

And then the lanterns!

Ah Nom had never seen so many. The huge one hanging in the center attracted her more than all the rest, for in it were funny little men and women holding hands. When the heated air arose from the candle inside it made them all fly around in the most comical way.

This was even better than watching the priests, and Ah Nom began to beg, "Hep me up! I likee see funny men."

"What, lift you?" said the lady, "Why you are too big. I can't lift you."

"No—I not big; I velly littoo (little). Please!" she smiled back. The lady lifted her, and was rewarded by a real Chinese smile, which is as good as sunshine.

Just then, who should appear upon the scene but Leen Soy, the child to whom Ah Nom's father objected.

Leen Soy had a jealous disposition, and when she saw the lady whom she also loved holding Nom up to see the funny men, her anger knew no bounds. The pretty face grew sullen, and the pretty lips stuck out, while an angry scowl came upon the forehead. Could this be Leen Soy who was pulling at Nom, hitting her and crying, "Ah Nom no good; I no likee his; him velly bad."

This only delighted Nom the more, for there was great rivalry existing between herself and the other child, and just now she had the proud distinction of being the favored one.

When, however, Leen Soy had her turn,

the scowls disappeared, and the pretty face was radiant.

Peace was restored, and the children were hugging each other tightly, much to the amusement of the onlookers.

"Are n't they sweet?" "Did you ever see anything so cunning?" people were saying, when—Ah Nom's father appeared upon the scene.

His face was not nice to see when he discovered Ah Nom with the forbidden child, but the friend did all she could to put him in a good humor, and save the child from punishment.

Soon the lady had quite a crowd of Chinese children holding her hands and tugging at her skirts, but she did not mind this at all, because she loved them all.

"Where shall we go next?" she inquired.

"To the theater!" they replied in chorus, and away they rushed to the other end of the street, where an open air theater was erected.

The actors and orchestra were one and the same. They had all been hired for the occasion, and were evidently doing their best to earn their money. The two end ones were beating on queer *lau gwoo* (drums); another was clashing the huge *chow* (cymbals), and the other was banging away on the *di lau* (tom-tom).

The rest of the instruments hung on the table, to be used when necessary. Above this table were the familiar gods and goddesses.

Plays were given every afternoon and night, to the delight of throngs of people who crowded around. The actors made such funny faces, and their voices were so high and squeaky, as they tried to imitate a high caste lady, that it made all the American people laugh.

"Above this table were the familiar Gods and Goddesses."

When the children grew tired, the lady took them home, for they could not sit up to see the "burning of the devil." This would not take place until three o'clock in the morning, so they went to bed, Ah Nom too weary to remember either sorrow or gladness.

While it was still dark she awoke, and peeping from the iron barred window saw—something that made her timid heart almost stop beating.

The darkness of the night was illumined with torches, and there was a great noise, which had awakened her. So benumbed was her brain with the deep sleep of childhood that she did not at first realize what it was—this hideous creature with staring eyes and horrible features, so, frightened, she crouched trembling in the darkness, until she remembered.

It was Di See the mighty! Di See—king of all the devils. Hastily bowing her tired head she did homage to the ugly thing, for she was only an ignorant little heathen child.

The priests were there, and all the male inhabitants of Chinatown, for Di See had to be carried all over the quarter, while they paused at every corner, put him down, and worshiped him. After this he was placed on a huge bonfire and burned. Then he was supposed to go back to the devils, and, by telling them how nicely he had been treated, cause them to leave the Chinese people alone for a year.

The lady did not sleep at all that night. Instead, she kept vigil in the house where the telephone was, and never took her eyes from Ah Nom's home.

Shortly before the burning of Di See a carriage deposited some guests at the back door of the house where the lady kept vigil. Some one was evidently watching for these visitors, who were whisked inside, no one being the wiser. Two big American people saw the arrivals, but they kept their own counsel.

Some one else must have come on the same train, for early that morning a stranger was seen to enter the door of Nom's house. The lady, who was peeping from a tiny window across the street, knew that this person was a highbinder, because he wore an elegant silk blouse with embroidered buttons, grayish-blue trousers, rather tight fitting, his hair being done in a very loose queue. He had a face like a fox—a face not to be trusted.

Ah Nom was awakened quite early that morning, and arrayed in her best garments. She was a trifle pale, but exquisite as a pomegranate blossom. She had for the moment forgotten that this was the day she was to be sold, but the lady friend could not forget, and there were others who remembered.

It was unfortunate that the police should

come in at the back door just as the highbinder was closing his bargain for the child, and was in the very act of placing his money on the teakwood table.

No one ever knew how the officers opened the door, but then you know they are privileged characters, and have a right to raid a gambling house whenever they please.

It seemed odd, too, that when they had entered they should walk straight to the front door and open it, when—who should come stepping in, as calmly and pleasantly as if attending an afternoon tea, but—"The Tiger" and Ah Ching.

Ah Nom stood trembling, watching it all as one watches a play, and fearing every moment that something terrible would happen. But The Tiger looked the highbinder in the face while she put her arms about the child, and said (interpreting through Ah Ching):

"Your father would sell you into a living

death, my child, so I have come to save you."

Ah Ching recognized the highbinder as one who had frequented the opium house where she had lived as a slave, but she knew he had no power to harm her now.

Ah Nom gazed at the young interpreter, and feeling reassured seemed to try to read The Tiger's face for one moment. Then, with a child's unerring instinct, she crept into her arms, and together they left the house.

CHAPTER FOURTEEN

THE RAIN FAIRIES

AH CHING in her old life had hated the rainy days, but now that she lived in the Home, where everything was bright and cheery, she was really glad to see them.

In California there was no rain during the summer, but it usually started in about September, cooling the parched earth, and making everything fresh and fragrant. This first rain of the season was quite welcome to all the girls, for it meant the doing of delightful and unusual things, such as making candy, popping corn, etc. On stormy days they all seemed to prefer the big, cheerful kitchen to any other part of the house.

"Beautiful Cloud."

But while these girls who were protected and loved, and whose lives were happy ones, were having their good times in the kitchen, they thought and talked a great deal of the less fortunate ones, who had nothing cheerful in their lives, and who had no cause to love the rainy days.

There had been no rescues for some time—not since Ah Nom had been brought from San José. That had been in June, and it was now September.

The rain still came down in torrents, and the big giant Wind from the ocean rushed into the city of San Francisco, whirling like mad through the Chinese quarter. He blew his strong breath at the rain, tossing it into a silvery mist, and dashed it in a slanting way against the feet and umbrellas of the passersby.

Quite as slanting were the velvet eyes of Choy Won (beautiful cloud) as she pressed her small heathen nose against the iron grating of the door, gazing with all her might at everything within her limited area, and longing with all the intensity of a starved nature to be out in the storm, and to be part of it all.

She had always, in a childish, unformed way, felt her kinship with nature, and loved it in its wildest moods, though she had never been free to indulge this fancy.

She had her dreams, even though she were a little slave, bought in China and sold in America. She was too young, however, to realize the horror of being sold.

Sometimes the child had vague, indistinct recollections of at one time having been loved and caressed by some nameless being who was soft and enchanting—some one who seemed always to breathe forth the delicate fragrance of sandal wood and almond blossoms. Who it was she could not have told. She only knew that when she heard the word "mother" it seemed to recall the memory of this sweet person of mystery.

From her small barred window she had seen many strange things, and when she had poked her head from the door wonderful vistas of people and things had passed before her astonished gaze.

When she saw other girls walking the street she would say to herself, "I wish I could run on the street. Inside the house there is nothing but *fan-tan* and the smell of opium—and the gods. I hate it all—I hate it all!"

She said this in English sometimes, for when no one was listening she liked to use the little English at her command, as it seemed to bring her in touch with another world. She had picked up a little of this strange language from some of the men who came to play *fan-tan*. She did not know that any one in the world thought it wrong to play *fan-tan;*

nor did she know that any one deemed it harmful to smoke opium, because, you see, she had been among these things so long and there had been no one to tell her the truth.

And now, gazing wistfully at the storm, she murmured aloud, "Old bars, why do you shut me in from it all? I would like to see the rain fairies!"

"I think so heap *gowsi* (pretty) ladies live in the water allee same as the moon. . . . I know—I know—I will go and ask the joss to open the door for me!"

Suiting the action to the word, she ran back into the dark, opium-scented place.

The white candles always used in gambling houses were burning before the altar on the floor. Choy Won, however, did not like to kneel here, for the men who were playing *fan-tan* might laugh at her for worshiping the idols at this time of day, when even a child should know that four o'clock in the afternoon was the sacred dinner hour of the Chinese and the proper time for all to worship the idols.

So, flitting hastily through the fearsome place, she passed into the next room—the room where she ate and slept and lived and had her being, under the watchful eyes of an old woman who had charge of her.

This old woman was called a nurse, but was in reality the keeper of this slave girl—Choy Won. The name meant "beautiful cloud." Perhaps that was why the child always felt herself a part of the storm, and knew that the wildness of the elements responded to something similar in her own nature.

If the old woman had been at home, Choy Won would not have dared to pray at this unheard-of hour, but fortunately the *ah mo* had gone on an errand that day, and when this happened she always met other women of her caliber, with whom she would gabble by the hour.

Choy Won fell on her knees in front of the paper god hung on the wall, and touching her head three times to the strip of matting spread before his hideous majesty, she addressed him in her queer little heathen way: "Please open the iron barred door for me! I am a cloud," she whispered, "and want to get out with the other clouds."

She told him of her belief in the Rain Fairies, but on that point, or on any point, he vouchsafed no information.

Hastily jumping up, she now ran to see if it was time for the petition to be answered. With all her childish force she pulled and tugged at the door, and was just going to give up in despair, when—something wonderful happened.

Some would have said it was the idol; Choy Won believed it to be Rain Fairies. At any rate, SOMETHING made the door fly open, while great gusts of rain swept in, as if endeavoring to purify with their moist breath the foul atmosphere of the place.

The sea breezes, mist laden, were very enchanting to a little shut-in maid who was never allowed the privilege of breathing pure air, and to her they seemed as a breath from heaven. She really did not intend to take advantage of the freedom the Rain Fairies had bestowed upon her, but meant to be very good, and stay next the door, or else it might close suddenly and shut her out in the cold. Then the old woman would return and find that she had gone out, and she did not like to think what the result would be if this should happen.

So she contented herself with jumping up and down with glee, and poking her dear inquisitive nose up against the shop windows which were nearest her. There were wonderful things in those shop windows—things she had never seen before, and which were so pleasing that they surely must have come from the "moon goddess," or the gracious white rabbit who inhabited the moon.

After awhile she sat down in the doorway, watching the crowds as they passed. Who were all these people, anyway? If only, out of the whole big crowd, she could have just one *pong yow*, (friend) she mused, she would not desire anything more.

It seemed odd for such a charming child not to have one friend. Now that she pondered on it it seemed very odd, very sad, too.

Her thoughts wandered unconsciously to that vague, mysterious person with the delicate fragrance of sandal wood and almond blossom. Who could it have been? And why did the storm always seem to bring her back? Whoever it was, must in some way be connected with the rain fairies. Perhaps some day these fairies would bring this wonderful being back into her life; and she prayed aloud to them to bring her this one of fragrance—with a mouth like the pomegranate in its bloom, and hair like lacquer.

"O, bring her quick—quick!" she gasped. "I *must* be loved! I must have *pong yow*!" Speaking in English she had not thought of any one understanding, but—some one did.

This "some one" was an American lady, with eyes that were serious one moment and laughing the next. As she approached the spot where the slave child sat thus talking to herself, she paused, adjusting her umbrella and skirt, and the child caught these words: "Well, *ah mooie*, what are you doing here in the rain?"

How did this strange person know the familiar Chinese word "*ah mooie?*" (little sister) thought Choy Won, and was so taken by surprise that she almost forgot to reply. Encouraged, however, by the love in the kind eyes, she responded eagerly:

"I am looking for the Rain Fairies. I think maybe they will bring me a *pong yow.*"

"Who knows but they have brought you a *pong yow?*" replied the stranger; "Will you let me be your *pong yow, samen jai?*"

There were the Chinese words again. What could it mean? She had not known that any American lady could speak the Chinese language.

"How did you learn to speak English?" the new friend now interrogated; for she was equally surprised to find that this small celes tial maiden could speak it so well.

"The men who come to play *fan-tan*—they teachee me—I likee." She smiled, and hung her flower-like head in shyness at having spoken so freely to a stranger.

But some way this lady did not seem like a stranger, for she had a way of understanding things, as if she had known one always.

Could it be, the child pondered, that she might know the Rain Fairies? Might even be one?

The lady of understanding hugged her up tightly as she said tenderly:

"Would you like me to be one, dear?"

"'*Ngau seung!*" (I would) responded the child. "I be very glad."

"All right then, *ah mooie;* be it understood that from this time on I am a Rain Fairy. I will be anything that makes you happy and —free."

Choy Won clapped her hands for very joy, as she realized that she had at last found a friend.

Meanwhile the lady wrinkled her brows as if struck by a sudden thought, and gazing curiously at the child, said:

"Do you live with your father and mother here?"

"No, no! I no got faddeh and moddeh. I no *sabé*. Olo woman she keep me—olo man he allee time play *fan-tan* and *pie gow*. I not go outside; I allee time stay in housee. Sometime olo woman velly closs (cross) to me. I no *sabé* anything."

"What is your name, child?" now eagerly interrupted the lady. "Tell me quickly!"

"Me name?—Choy Won!—beautiful cloud—" replied the child.

With a great cry of joy the lady grasped the cold little hand, saying, "That is the name. Surely it must be—it must be."

Meanwhile it was growing dark, and the lanterns were being lighted, throwing out their pale yellow gleams into the misty night of storm.

What if the old woman should return and find her *protégée* talking to the Rain Fairy?

She would surely beat her to death, and then she would never, never see the good fairy again.

Glancing apprehensively into the growing darkness, she ventured, "I think so olo lady come plitty soon. Just now I go—come again, when the Rain Fairies open the door."

But the newly-found friend was not to be dismissed so easily, and hurriedly whispered:

"Little one, listen to me! Do you know you are the very child for whom I have been seeking for months? You must come with me at once! I will tell you all about it later, but now—only come!"

She must surely obey the Rain Fairy, who had been the only one to speak a kind word to her. After all, she reflected, she hated with all the intensity of her soul both the old highbinder who owned her and the old hag who guarded her; so why should she not obey the good Rain Fairy? It was the right thing to do—she knew it was, and without a look at the place which had held her a prisoner, she slipped away, holding fast to the protecting hand, and almost hidden by the great umbrella.

What matter if the rain did pour in torrents on the *pong yow* lady? The slave was hidden from her enemies, and the rain loved the lady, and the lady loved the rain.

It was cold outside, but at last they entered great doors from which streamed rays of cheery light, and when once inside, what was the child's astonishment to discover a big crowd of Chinese girls, who soon explained everything to her. She knew then that the lady was in reality the good fairy who made it her life work to rescue Chinese slave girls.

But best of all—this same lady had been away over in China, and knew "the mysterious person who smelled of sandal wood and almond blossoms," and bestest of all, that

"The mysterious person who smelled of sandal wood and Almond blossoms."

same fragrant personage, who was none other than Choy Won's mother—her very own mother—was sent for right away, and it was only a few short weeks until the child knew what it was to be loved and petted by a "really, truly mother"—one who was always redolent of the sacred sandal wood and almond blossom.

CHAPTER FIFTEEN

THANKSGIVING

FOR months the girls had been planning as to how they should celebrate the American Thanksgiving day, and the best part of it was that they did not think of their own pleasure, but of how they might brighten life for others.

People who are connected with rescue work have ways of finding out where the needy and suffering are, who do not often live in attractive places.

To one who was not interested in the suffering ones it might have seemed a fearsome thing to enter these forbidding places, which are usually reeking with dirt, but when one goes with a real love burning in the heart and a great desire to help the suffering and those in bondage, it is wonderful how even the meanest cellar home will be glorified and transformed.

Thanksgiving Eve had come at last.

That was a busy time in the Rescue Home. The door bell was kept ringing almost constantly, for the American friends, too, had been admitted to the great secret and were sending in donations of all kinds.

Ah Ching had never before known what Thanksgiving was, so, in order that she might enjoy its pleasures to the full, she was allowed to answer the door. This was a great pleasure to her, as a Chinese girl is always filled with curiosity, and to have the privilege of opening the door and receiving the messages and parcels was surely better than peeping over the banisters with the other girls.

It was a pleasure not only to Ah Ching,

but also to the ones who rang the bell, for so soft and sweet were the manners of Miss Cameron's girls, and so gentle and refined were they, showing such courtesy to every one, that it was always a joy to meet them, after having been accustomed to blustering American ways.

Ah Ching was fairly bubbling over with joy, and her eyes were aglow with delight. Few would have recognized in her the poor slave who had been rescued several months before.

The girl never knew what was going to come next, and her cold hands trembled with excitement every time she cautiously opened the great iron door. This door had always to be opened cautiously, because no one could ever tell who might be outside, waiting for an opportunity to rush in and recapture some of the girls. Wicked people were always lying in wait to regain their prizes.

But when once the big iron door on Sacramento Street had closed and shut in the slave, it was indeed a difficult thing for the fiends to get their clutches upon her.

"The Tiger" lived behind this door—The Tiger who was all love and kindness for her dear slave girls, and who was only a gentle lady with a big heart full of love, after all.

Ah Ching needed all the English at her command that day. Every time the door bell rang her sandals would go tapping over the polished floors, and after receiving the package she would go to the proper person and deliver it with explanations. Many of the donations were for the Mission itself, and others for the poor and needy, whom the girls were planning to surprise.

The cool sea breeze forced its way in at the door every time it was opened, and its salt breath was always sweet to the girls, for somehow it seemed to speak of freedom. The cold air made the Home seem all the more cozy when it brought its hint of what the outside world was like.

That night the girls did not like to take time even for supper, but preferred to peep from all sorts of places when the bell rang.

Still, a crowd of hungry girls can always do justice to a meal, and to-night they made an unusually attractive picture as they sat at the little round table, eating Chinese food in Chinese fashion, chop-sticks and all.

Bed time came, and their last thoughts were of the morrow and its pleasures. All slept sweetly, secure in their refuge, for was not the great door bolted and barred against all intruders? and was not The Tiger always there, ready to protect them—with her life, if need be?

It had been decided to start out quite early, as something delightful was to happen

"Holding each other's hands, to keep from slipping on the cobbles."

at the Home later in the day, and they must return in plenty of time for this event.

Only a few girls were allowed to accompany the teacher, because if certain ones were seen they might be snatched up by the ever watchful enemy and spirited away through the devious, underground passages, and back to a life of slavery. The Tiger never took any chances with the highbinders.

At last they started out through the narrow streets, holding each other's hands, to keep from slipping on the cobbles. The Chinese people stared at them as they passed, for to them the sight of a *mooie jai* was always full of interest.

The teacher led the gay little procession, ever keeping her eye on them, and holding by the hand a small brother of one of the girls. A wagon full of mysterious and many shaped and sized parcels followed them, and paused in front of each door they entered. The heathen people knew nothing of the "Melican Thanksgiving," and wondered vaguely what it was all about. It irritated some of them to see these pretty young girls walking the streets at this meaningless season, wearing gayly-colored robes, when it was neither the "Chinese New Year" nor yet the "devil feast."

How did they dare? They dared because The Tiger had set them free, and they no longer observed any heathen customs.

It was nothing to them if the men did mutter as they passed. The men knew, as well as they, that the big policeman who was sauntering so innocently half a block behind them had been appointed as their especial escort, and would lose no time defending them, if occasion required.

Away back in some of the homes pale mothers were peeping from dark recesses. Some of these mothers knew what it meant to have their own daughters sold as slaves, and their timid hearts rejoiced at the sight of the rescued ones, and they whispered:

"I am glad! I am glad for you, *mooie jai!*"

The first place to be entered was a rickety tenement, where lay an old lady with bound feet. She was a hopeless old mother who had been in her room for ten years, deserted by her children, and had never thought of receiving even a kind word again, much less the sack of rice and other Chinese eatables which these dear girls had the man carry up to her.

They told this shut-in soul all about the American God and the American Thanksgiving, and sang a hymn with Chinese words. The sweetness of it touched the rusty heartstrings of the old heathen woman, and she could not keep back the tears. She exulted on reflecting that these pure young beings had been rescued, and would be all right now, as she knew what the life was from which they had been snatched.

Down into a cellar home they next descended, unmindful of the close, opium-laden atmosphere; unmindful because they knew that the dear invalid mama of little Yoke Fun was lying there expecting them, but not expecting the great rice sack of provisions which they had brought.

Yoke Fun was a dear boy who came to the Mission school. He was discovered outside the patched-up door now, playing in an old basket with some small friends of his. As the girls approached he stood up and smiled broadly, for his prophetic soul told him that something pleasant was going to happen. Something pleasant always did happen when the Mission girls came, and to him, as to many others, they were as ministering angels.

Yoke Fun was well named, for in spite of all their poverty he was always ready to laugh, and to hear the jolly laugh was always better than medicine to his mother.

"As the girls approached he stood up and smiled broadly."

They had been over from China only one year, but the boy had learned English so rapidly that he laughed at the other boys when they called string "stling," and American "Melican."

Now he ran on in front of them, to impart the glad news that they were coming. He was always very fond of showing his dear "*ah ma*" what excellent English he could speak.

"*Ah ma*," (mama) he cried, "I think so American Thanksgiving heap good day. Allee time pray to heaven—eat big dinner."

His boyish idea of it was that one must either pray or eat all day. The first was not so interesting, but the latter appealed to him, for like most boys of that age, he was blessed with a good appetite.

The shut-in mama seemed to like best of all the bunch of violets, and buried her pale face in their great purple hearts, inhaling their fragrance.

Ah Ching interpreted for her as she said to the teacher:

"*Nay jon hai ho sum; daugea nay.*" (You are very kind; I thank you!)

It was afternoon before the errands of love were quite finished, and the tired but happy girls hastened back to the Home, which was indeed home to them.

When they entered, hungry from their long walk, savory odors assailed them, and there were joyful whispers, and stealthy closing of the doors which led into the dining room. Also, certain of the older girls were nowhere to be seen.

After a time—when it had seemed to some of the younger ones that they really could not wait another minute—something happened.

The dinner bell rang!

There was nothing so very unusual in that, as it did the same thing every day, but to-day was different, as Thanksgiving came but once a year.

The huge doors swung back, and there in the cheerful dining room was a feast fit even for the Moon Goddess.

But what to Ah Ching was the greatest surprise of all was, that a stranger stood inside the door, and took the seat of honor by "Mama." And this handsome stranger was not a stranger after all, but on closer inspection proved to be just—*the friend the Lanterns had sent!*

Ah Ching's face was a study, as she in her joy, and sweet suggestion of womanhood, forgot the old heathen custom that a girl should be neither seen nor heard, and ran eagerly to his side, saying:

"O, friend of myself and of the Lanterns! How can I thank you for what you have given me?—the new God—freedom—Mama—O, I *can not!*"

As she clung to his hands and he looked at her he thought how the little blossom was unfolding in the atmosphere of love, and wondered that he had not before noticed how very beautiful she was.

She would soon be a woman, he reflected.

And she, as she gazed at him, said in her heart:

"It is strange I did not before see how noble looking was this Lantern friend."

Then a sudden embarrassment fraught with sweetness seemed to fall upon her as a garment, and she withdrew her hand from his, and passed to her place among the other girls.

It was a real Thanksgiving dinner, and no mistake. Surely the kind friends of the Mission had been at work, for the table was heavily laden with good things.

Roast turkeys were there in abundance, for sixty hungry girls can eat a great deal on occasion.

And there were mince and pumpkin pie, fit even for the Empress of China to bite, and huge, steaming plum puddings, with a sprig of holly atop.

Cakes, too, were there, that must have been made by the fairies, or surely they could not have been so light and feathery. Perhaps the "moon fairies" had a hand in it; at least some of the younger ones thought so.

But what use to try and describe all the dainties at that table, or to tell of the continuous girlish chattering, intermingled with Chinese giggles in all keys? Nobody in the world could describe such joyous things as youth and happiness and freedom.

Afterward, there was much music and merriment, and perhaps the one who enjoyed it most of all—because to him it was all so new and wonderful, was—the friend the Lanterns had sent.

CHAPTER SIXTEEN

IN THE TEMPLE OF LUNG GONG

THE Eve of the birthday of the Christ-Child had come! But what did the heathen people in the great Chinese quarter of San Francisco know of it? Some of them had heard, but only vaguely remembered the cause of it all, nor dreamed what it meant to the civilized world. To them it meant only one thing, and that was that it wonderfully increased their sales of articles suitable for gifts.

With the coming of Christmas-tide the people of San Francisco poured into the Chinese quarter in throngs, and on a lofty balcony a little Chinese slave leaned over and gazed with her soul in her eyes at these strange people passing far below. To her imaginative mind the crowd seemed like a huge dragon, wriggling in and out of the crooked thoroughfares, but she did not fear this dragon. She loved it, and longed to be a part of its glittering, joyous body. It was its joyousness which most appealed to this little shut-in piece of girlhood.

This child, Ah Fah, was like a pure flower growing in a muddy pond. "Ah Fah" meant "the flower," and as she leaned and looked she resembled a pure, golden-hearted lily, drooping on its stem. Her delicately tinted loveliness was enhanced by the lavender *sohm* and gay hair ornaments she wore, but there was a sad reason for her rich attire on this occasion. To-night—this very night—her master was to take her to a certain place and show her to a highbinder who was to look at her with a view to purchase. This other highbinder was afraid to come to the man's house, as he had reason to believe that the place was being watched, and so they selected a very innocent spot for the meeting. It was —the temple of Lung Gong!

The girl did not know why she was going. The master had told her that as it was the American Christmas he had decided to take her upon the streets, so that she might see the people and the shops, and then to the temple, where she could offer up thanks to the idols for her unusual privileges.

Therefore she mused, "Now I am almost sorry I have hated him. After all, he may have a kind heart, and it is only that I have not understood." So she tried for a time to banish from her the memory of the cruelty he had shown her, and how she had been a captive, almost as high up as the sky, when she had hardly known whether to reach up to the glittering stars in entreaty or down to the lantern-decked streets below. So very long had she prayed to the idols, and with no results.

She had just about decided to supplicate the stars and the lanterns when this wonderful thing happened, and she thought that, after all, perhaps the "mother goddess" had relented and had decided to give her a little pleasure.

It was early yet, and it seemed to her the time would never come when she could step out of her cage and go for a few tantalizing hours into freedom. Inside this home there were no indications of Christmas, and as she looked around she seemed to see it all so differently, and hated, with a child's impulsive and unreasoning hate, every detail of it.

An old woman, with large green earrings and brown, hard face, sat sewing on a hand machine, making Chinese garments for the shops. A silver bird held in its unmusical mouth the narrow strip of cloth which was gradually evolving into a Chinese button. The old woman puffed vigorously at a cigarette while she sewed, and gave vent to her feelings in ill-natured remarks to the poor slave girls who were under her care; for others were there beside Ah Fah, but none so delicately beautiful as she. These other slaves were making cigarettes by the hundred, for all the people who ate his rice and drank his tea must make money for the avaricious master, whose only god was gold.

On the wall were the paper gods he pretended to worship, and it was the duty of the slaves to keep the punks burning before these idols, and the bowls of fresh food set before them.

The clock, which is never absent from a Chinese room, and is held sacred by celestials, pointed to the hour of eight. The time would soon come now, and the child's heart almost jumped out of her body with a strange excitement and prescience of some joy to come.

In the room below a game of "*pi-gow*" was in progress, and the excited voices of the men ascended to the child, seeming to shut out for a moment all the rose-hued dreams which were filling her brain. The odor of opium came up in gusts every time the door was opened. Her poor soul revolted at it all, and she said to the "mother goddess" on the wall, not audibly, but in a vicious little whisper: "I hate *pi-gow*—I hate opium—I hate the old woman and the master—I hate it all—all!"

The other girls wondered sadly why they were not to be allowed to go upon the streets as well as Ah Fah. They did not know the reason, but the old woman did, and chuckled fiendishly to herself, as she thought of the price the master would get for this beauty and—the commission she herself would receive when the sale was completed. For had she not told the new man about the slave and of her wondrous beauty? She had not consented to tell the master who the man was until he had given her his written promise to pay her a certain sum when the bargain should be finished.

This, then, was the cause of her vicious chuckling. She only thought of the gold she would soon have, and how she would take it and go back to China to buy more slaves, and thus she would soon accumulate a great deal of the shining ore for which men and women sell their souls. She had neither thought nor tenderness for the motherless child who was to be sold into a life worse than death—that side of it never occurred to her.

At last came the sound of the master's feet shuffling up the stairway. How familiar the sound, and how the slave girls hated it. How they trembled when they heard him, and ceased their girlish chatter and conjecture as to the whys and wherefores of life, and the strange part they took in it all.

Seung Chan was sly and stooped, and had the opium pallor. As he had never been known to do a kindly act, the girl could not understand the unexpected solicitude for the pleasure of the slave, nor why he should single her out from the others. They did not know, but he did, and so did the old hag and the other highbinder.

Meanwhile Ah Fah was trying not to show her happiness, for, if she did, he might decide not to take her; but having for so long had all childish delight denied her, and all desire for pleasure pent up in her heart, it seemed that she could not conceal the fact that she was happy, and her eyes danced, while the smiles and dimples played hide and seek on her pretty face.

He held the child's hand as they went

down the stairway. How she longed to free herself from the hated clasp, but dared not try. Soon she could see at close range the moving, sinuous crowd forming the great human dragon upon which she had gazed from her lofty abode; and now she—Ah Fah, the slave—was to become a part of this joyous, glittering thing, which really, upon close inspection, did not look like a dragon, but was far more beautiful and far more real, when one was a part of it. She had never felt half so important as now, as she walked along, herself an exquisite part of the beautiful mosaic of color.

The very spirit of Christmas was in the air, and the child felt it all, but could give no name to this wondrous joy and exhilaration which seemed to pulse through the cool, sea-laden air, and laugh from the lips of the throng. These people were not slaves. They were free, and they were happy!

Many were the wonderful sights of that walk. The gay bazaars of Sing Fat and other Chinese merchants were filled with a chattering, jolly crowd, buying gifts for Christmas.

Above Ah Fah's head swayed rows of joss lanterns, like globes of golden light, irradiating the darkness, and making a perfect fairy land of the scene.

And so the child walked on, nor dreamed what awaited her.

In the Rescue Home that night was a visitor—a lady from Menlo Park; a suburban place of residence for wealthy business men of San Francisco. This lady was possessed of millions, but lacked what would have meant more to her than the millions, and that was—a child! Miss Cameron had allowed Ah Ching to go shopping with this lady and the Lantern Friend, who happened also to be calling at the Home that evening. Mama knew that she could trust the girl with both these true and tried friends, and Ah Ching felt very happy and free as she went through the rich bazaars, while the lady bought gifts for her, and for many American friends.

The Lantern Friend was lifted up into a new world as he gazed at Ah Ching and noted how she had grown, and at last acknowledged to himself that his regard for her was very deep.

Meanwhile the master and Ah Fah had arrived at the temple of Lung Gong. The child had gazed in awe at the immense joss lanterns which swung on the balcony far above her, and with feelings of fear and wonder climbed the long flight of steps that led to the august presence of the five idols in the holy of holies. What would these mighty idols think of a worthless slave venturing to appear before them? Would they frown upon her? Would she dare offer up her simple little prayer to them, so great and high?

When she entered the sacred room all was a blaze of light. The rich teakwood chairs which lined the sides of the rooms were decked with red satin coverings, richly embroidered in gold. Rare carvings of brass and wood were everywhere, and huge panels with black letters covered the walls. These had been given to the temple with a large sum of money by wealthy people, and when one read the Chinese name, one was always supposed to remember who gave the panel—and the money.

At the front end of the long room was a curtained-off place, with rich carvings and large square teakwood lanterns. Here one could have a sup of tea, or, if one were Chinese, a puff at the opium pipe, while reclining on the bamboo couches. This room led to the picturesque balcony outside, where one might stand and look down upon thousands of swaying lanterns and throngs of people. It was all very attractive, but the most important part was the gaudy altar whereon sat in majesty the five idols, their heads gay with red and gold paper ornaments, from which flaunted the ubiquitous peacock feather.

The other highbinder was on time, and sauntered up to them as they entered. As the child did not know their plans, she thought nothing of this until the man began to look upon her critically and pronounce upon her seeming defects. Why should it concern this man? Surely it could make no difference to him if she were this or if she were that. Soon the two men walked on into the tea room, the master bidding the child worship the idols for a few moments. This was the chance of a lifetime for her. Kwan Yum had never answered her petitions. Perhaps these new gods might?

As she bowed her pretty head upon the strip of matting spread for that purpose, she prayed, "Please give me a Mama of my very own!"

This was interesting to the lady from Menlo, who with her friends had just entered, and were admiring the gayly-decked altar while the little one was speaking aloud to the gods. A blue-coated policeman who was also watching it was not only amused, but suddenly interested—vitally interested; and with the Lantern Friend for interpreter, quickly interrogated the child in a low tone. Certain instructions were given to the child, who promised to be very quiet, no matter what happened. It chanced that this very officer was out on a quest that night, and fate must have led him to this spot. He had a right to capture a slave at any time.

The child now glanced fearfully in the direction of the two highbinders. They could not see her companions, who were concealed by a tall screen.

What if the master should find that she had been talking to strangers? He would surely punish her.

Well, the bargain was at last completed! The two plotters had just turned to come back, one to claim his new property, and the other to go home and give the commission to the old hag, who was eagerly awaiting him.

Suddenly—the lights went out, and the place of the *joss* was in total darkness. No one knew how it chanced, except—the policeman. He had made a study of the electric buttons in Chinatown, and had a right to turn them on and off when he saw fit.

The lady from Menlo had reached the foot of the stairway before the lights went out. Her carriage stood waiting. In a second's time the big, kindly officer had the trembling slave in his arms, and was down the steps and had placed her in the carriage. The highbinders above were searching madly

"Did the five idols smile joyously, or was it imagination?"

for their prey, uttering all sorts of imprecations, and searching even under the joss altar.

Did the five idols smile joyously, or was it imagination?

The child was the very one for whom the police had for months been seeking. She was an orphan—the lady was childless, and so—that night in the mansion at Menlo Park there was for the first time a pair of child's stockings hanging by the fireplace. Even if they were short Chinese stockings, Santa Claus would know them.

The woman had found something to fill the empty place in her heart, and the child had found—a Mama—of her "very own," in the temple of Lung Gong!

CHAPTER SEVENTEEN

THE FIRST CHRISTMAS OF AH PING

CHRISTMAS was to mean something this time to more than one slave, and while happy preparations were going on in the Home, the good Christmas Fairy was at work in the great Chinatown.

Ah Ping had never known what Christmas was. She dimly remembered that when she was living in China, in the old, care-free days, she had heard something about the birth of the Christ-Child; but none of its real meaning penetrated her brain.

"Is there anything good or happy in the whole big world?" she murmured plaintively; but there was none to answer.

There had been a time, away back in

China, when the little face had known a mother's kiss, and she had been free to do as a child's heart dictates; but the mother died, and Ah Ping was sold to a Chinese man and his wife, who came to America and settled in the San Francisco Chinatown. From that time on, although her name meant "peace," there was no more peace for Ah Ping. So on this same eventful Christmas Eve, in the dark upper story of a Chinese tenement house, Ah Ping was out on a balcony, communing with herself.

"I am glad I have myself to talk to," she said, "because there is no one else, and I am so lonely—O, so lonely!" How her innocent heart longed for something; a mother's love, a kind word, some one who cared.

"Perhaps it is only because I do not understand. Perhaps every one is lonely and unhappy. O, big *joss*, let me die! Let me get away from it all!"

Far down on the narrow streets she could dimly watch the hurrying crowds, who looked as if they might be happy, and seemed really free. "I would like to be free," she said; "Maybe next time I shall be; maybe—I no can tell."

The world of "little China" was beautiful at night, when the shadows hid the unpleasant places, and the great lanterns of the *joss* glowed in rows on the flower-laden balconies and in front of the doors, whereon were inscribed happy greetings to all who should enter. It looked beautiful to one who saw only the surface, and did not dream of the slavery and bondage underlying it. It would not have seemed so to one who had seen the pitiful little slave girls doing the bidding of the old hags who guarded them, and being punished at any time, whether busy or idle.

It was Christmas Eve. Ah Ping knew it, because she had heard her master and mistress talking of it; but it was nothing to her. She would be unhappy just the same on Christmas day as on any other day; so why should she rejoice over the birthday of the Christ-Child? But even as she sat thinking and talking to herself, her mistress had awakened from her deep opium sleep, and rushing out to the balcony grasped her frail little arm. For some reason she was more cruel than usual. Perhaps she feared the child would get some Christmas joy into her life.

At any rate, Ah Ping went to her couch with bruised body and breaking heart, and after every one was asleep, crept out of bed, and felt around in the darkness for something with which to put an end to this life of slavery and suffering. She had once heard of a slave girl committing suicide by drinking *pow fah*, (a hair dressing used by Chinese ladies) so why could she not do the same? There was no need for her to live—no one wanted her;

she was only fit to be beaten and abused. And who could tell? Perhaps in the next life she might be happy; might possibly be one of the lovely maidens in the moon, whose office it was to pound rice continually for the concoction of wonderful cakes for good children. At least it was worth trying; so the poor little half-crazed thing crept to the jar where the poison was, and giving one last long glance downward at the lantern-hung streets, and then upward where the Christmas stars twinkled in the darkness, she grasped the jar and drained its contents.

"Now! I shall be free!" she gasped, and lay down, expecting to die. The dose, however, was not sufficiently strong, or something was the matter, for instead of going into oblivion, she grew deathly sick. Her master and mistress were aroused, and all was confusion. They did not want to lose a valuable slave, so gave her some Chinese drugs, and she recovered.

THE FIRST CHRISTMAS OF AH PING

Through the little bird which hovers over Chinatown, as well as over other places, the news, by some strange chance, reached the ears of Miss Cameron that very next morning—Christmas morning. So, when the bells were ringing out their merry chimes, and peace was on the earth and in the air, Miss Cameron, in company with an officer and Ah Ching, started out on her errand of mercy.

Reaching the place, they climbed the narrow, tortuous steps. There was no light save that which came up through the street door, but they were accustomed to finding their way in dark places. Almost any one would have been frightened to death, yet these brave people went as calmly as if they were going to a tea party. They knew just where to go, for the little bird had told them, and at last reached the top story of the tenement house where lived Ah Ping.

Nothing could be seen but a blank-looking door, with a small grated opening near the top. Ah Ching said in Chinese, "We want to come in!" Then the cruel mistress opened a tiny crack in the door, that she might hear more clearly. That gave the rescuers just the chance they desired, and, without any ceremony, they all rushed in, searching hastily in every direction for the poor little slave girl.

Noise and confusion reigned! Everything was a perfect uproar, and all who lived in that part of the tenement seemed to be in the fight.

What chance could the poor child have, with so many against her? From all sides came low Chinese mutterings and imprecations. Ah Ching's heart almost stood still, but she called as loudly as she could, through all the din and confusion:

"*Ping Ah! Ping Ah! 'ngau nay lie gow nay!*" (We have come to save you!)

The joyous message penetrated the mysteries of the place, and from a dark passageway came the sound of an opening door, while from this door peeped, O, so cautiously, the pale, sad face of the one they sought. The excitement now became intense.

"Little fool!" hissed the mistress; "Do n't you know they have come to kill you? They will take you and break your bones; they will boil your eyes—they will—"

But somehow the child's heart knew, and she looked intently at Miss Cameron, and saw real love shining from her eyes and real tears of pity dropping from them, as with outstretched hands she advanced toward the child.

Ah Ching whispered, "That must be the one we want," and without a moment's hesitation the big strong policeman reached down tenderly, and, catching the frightened child in his kind arms, started for the doorway.

Meanwhile perfect pandemonium reigned! The Chinese were beside themselves with rage. Should they stand calmly by and see a three thousand dollar slave torn from their grasp? In their anger they tried every way to drag the child from the officer's arms, but all to no avail. He knew his business, and he was big and strong, and was fighting for the right. With one mighty effort he released himself from the clutches of the many yellow hands tugging at him, and dashed out at the door, down the narrow steps, and into pure air. Ah Ping lay trembling in the protecting arms.

They had to go first to the city prison, as the law required it. Although the officials were accustomed to sad and strange sights, they were touched by the pathetic figure of Ah Ping, with bare, dirty feet and straggling locks. There were no dry eyes while the little one was telling her sad story, and stopping every few moments to inquire of the sweet-faced Ah Ching, "Are you *sure* they will not beat me at the Mission?" On being assured that no beating awaited her, she said, "O, take me there quickly, then, before they find me!"

* * * * *

Christmas festivities at the Home were to be held on the day after Christmas this year, and so the girls were all busily engaged in the delightful task of preparing for the great occasion when the new child entered the Mission. The door bell was kept tingling constantly, and mysterious packages of all sizes and shapes were smuggled into the house, and slipped into a certain room, the door of which had been locked for several days. No one but Miss Cameron and a favored few were allowed to enter this room, and many were the whispered consultations held outside this door, and the joyous speculation among the tiny ones as to what might be in there.

There were many things in the Home which Ah Ping had never known. She was given a bath and placed in a clean, warm bed, where she soon forgot her sorrow in sleep.

When she awoke, feeling like a new being, she was given some lovely Chinese garments, and when she looked in a mirror she hardly knew herself. After awhile she heard a bell ring. Somehow it had a delightful sound, and suggested all sorts of pleasant things. She did not know what it meant until Miss Cameron came to her and said, "Come to your first Christmas dinner, little one;" and holding tightly the slim fingers of the gentle lady, she entered the dining room, full of chattering girls. In the center of the room was a long table on which there was surely everything in the world to eat. Several big turkeys were there, for these girls had excellent appetites, and there were innumerable other dainties, for the Rescue Home had many

"When she looked in a mirror she hardly knew herself."

kind friends who always remembered them generously on these occasions. There was such an air of peace and good will that the tired stranger soon lost all fear, and felt herself one of them.

She rested in peace that evening, while Mama and some of the girls went to a Christmas tree at a church. What that might mean she did not know as yet.

CHAPTER EIGHTEEN

THE CHRISTMAS STAR

ANOTHER little slave to whom Christmas meant nothing was Louey Ching. She was not supposed to indulge in the infantile luxury known as happiness. One needed only to glance at the cruel face and shrewd, shifting eyes of the old highbinder who owned her to know that he would not willingly confer happiness upon any one. To him happiness meant the buying and selling of pretty tea-rose maidens, and getting a good price for them.

So dazed was the *mooie jai* with the many undeserved cruelties she had received that she seemed to be conscious of but one thing, and that was her longing to get away. But

"Another little slave to whom Christmas meant nothing was Louey Ching."

how could she get away, when the front door was always locked, and the back door led only to some steps going up to the roof? She ran up these steps now and peered over the edge just to picture how it would be to jump off; but her lingering gaze brought into focus such a new world—such a radiant Christmas world—that it seemed a pity to end it all when there was a world like that below. If only she could get to it!

And now she dimly remembered hearing once that there was a "'Melican *Joss*" who would answer one's petitions when the idols failed. Why had this idea never occurred to her before? She would appeal to this new *Joss*—the sooner the better—so, lying flat on her little stomach she cried aloud and said: "Let me go into the new world! Let me never be beaten any more!"

When she came down stairs, and into the long Chinese room with its meager and dirty furnishings, she felt almost happy, for in her small heathen heart was the pure faith of a child.

It was growing dark. She must set fresh food before the gods, and attend to her duties, far too heavy for a child who should be at play. She must—what was it that made her heart almost stop beating, her face grow pale, and her eyes wide with pleased surprise? She had stepped on something, and—it was something which made her think that her prayer was going to be answered.

Nothing more nor less than the bunch of keys which had never before left the keeping of the old highbinder. In her small hand she now held freedom. He had gone, locking the door with the spring lock, and had forgotten the keys. It was too good to be true. The door was locked, and she—had the key to that lock. "*Daugea! daugea! wah may Joss!*" (Thank you! thank you! Beautiful God!) she hysterically sobbed; then, realizing there was not a moment to lose, she cast a hurried glance at the barren room and said, "I *hate* you, prison walls! I *hate* you, ugly old god! I am never going to come again. I am going to find the beautiful new God, who hears me when I talk to Him."

So saying, she hastily singled out the right key, for she had taken careful note of it many times, and had hated the slender thing which shut her away from happiness and the freedom of childhood. Into the lock it went. O joy! it turned as easily as if it were glad to set the small prisoner free, and never, perhaps, did the turning of one key mean so much.

There was not a moment to lose—the old man might return at any time. Trembling with fear, she crept like a haunted thing down the rickety, foul-smelling stairway. A rat scurried under her feet, making her almost faint with fright. . . . She lived a lifetime until her sandaled feet touched the last step, and she emerged into the pure, untainted air of freedom.

She could feel there was something unusual in the air, although she did not know it was Christmas night. It was all so bright and pretty. She could not stop to see it, for she realized that she must get out of the Chinese quarter, or her master might find her. Straight on, therefore, she kept, and walked and walked, past gay Chinese shops, rich with Oriental treasures; past the *joss* temples and the huge *joss* lanterns, with their long, beckoning rays of light; past the shuttered and barred doors of underground homes, where she caught glimpses of other poor slaves, and on to something, she knew not what.

The night was cold and she was tired, for she was not accustomed to walking on the streets. She was out of Chinatown now, and instead of the smell of incense and opium, something very delightful greeted her nostrils. She looked up and saw men on the street corners, selling great bunches of violets, and from the flowers came this delicious perfume.

Glancing up at the sky she noticed one great star larger than the rest. It seemed to invite her and lead to something pleasant. "Perhaps it is a lantern the new God has lighted for me," she murmured. "At any rate I will let it guide me." And so the heathen child was led and guided by the Christmas star, and soon, through a window in a large building, she saw another star of light, and knew she had been directed to this place.

She almost feared to go in, as she was only a little Chinese girl who knew but a few words of the language of this strange people to whom the star was guiding her. Following the light, she entered a great building into which crowds of American people and many children were going. "Too muchee *samen jai*," she murmured. This must be heaven! Surely it could be nothing less, she reflected, for the inside air was warm and full of delightful perfume, and the velvet cushions seemed to embrace her tired body like the arms of love.

Melodious sounds were coming from somewhere—she had n't the least idea where—and she was almost afraid to look up, for fear some one would beat her, or put her out. The poor child did not know that it was the birthday of the "Jesus Baby" these people were celebrating. She did not know that the very spirit of the Christ-Child was in the air, and that in this huge church into which she had strayed there would be nothing but kind thoughts and deeds for her.

Finally she ventured to look up, and was now sure this was heaven. She must be dead, after all.

Away in front of her was a big, big tree,

all green and feathery looking. It seemed alive, and was covered with wonderful sparkles. She knew! It was the "tree of heaven!" She had heard of it before, and on its swaying branches she could see—*goon jai* (dolls)—dozens of them. She rubbed her eyes and pinched herself, but still could not believe she was really alive. She had never had a doll; she never expected to have one, but anyhow, she was very glad to have the privilege of looking at them. It would be something she could always remember.

Just at this point in her reflections a soft hand was laid upon her own cold one, and a soft voice which sounded like pretty music said to her, "Are you all alone, dear?" "*Hi lah!*" she responded. The lady knew that meant yes, and placing one protecting arm around her, said, "Then come with me, and we will sit near the front, where you can see the tree." The child did not understand all the words, but felt the love in them, and clinging closely to her new friend, she was led up the carpeted aisle and given a seat close—close to the wonderful "tree of heaven."

But what was most wonderful was, that when she was seated she found herself in the presence of other Chinese girls, as well as American ones. What could it mean? The lady smiled at her questioning eyes, and listened eagerly while the Chinese girls interrogated the little one. She soon told them her pitiful story, and the lady answered softly, "Little one, the Christmas Star must have brought you to us, for all these other dear ones are rescued slaves, and I am their American Mama. You also shall go and live with us, where the old highbinder can never find you.

The child's heart was too full for utterance, but the radiant face and tear-filled eyes were better than words to one who knew and loved the Chinese girls, and the kind lady understood. The girls were so good, and glad to explain the meaning of it. While they whispered their few words of explanation the music grew louder and grander, until it seemed as if the heart of the child would burst for very ecstasy.

Looking high up, she now saw for the first time the great shining star which she thought had guided her to the place. It must be the same; and now it was resting, radiant, scintillating, on the topmost bough of the "tree of heaven," and just beneath it, swaying gently, was the figure of the Christ-Child, and it held out its arms, pink and dimpled, and seemed to beckon to the rescued one.

While she looked, some one took a *goon jai* from the tree of glitters and gave it to Louey Ching. She could not believe it. She? the poor slave child with a *goon jai?* But the girls assured her there could be no mistake about the doll.

The Christ-Child seemed to smile at her, and she smiled back and said, "*Samen jai! samen jai! mea wah?*" (the child! the child! what is it?) And the girls replied, "It is the Christ-Child!"

The next day was a memorable one in the Home, for with a record of three rescues that Christmas, Mama felt that every one was entitled to a good time.

Soon after dinner the darkness fell, and then the whole crowd of eager, laughing girls were admitted into the mysteries of the room with the closed door. Entering its portals they saw a beautiful green tree which touched the ceiling, and on its topmost bough shone radiantly a great star. Brilliant lights sparkled all over the tree, and rich gifts hung from its branches.

"Is it really growing, and did the Christ-Child put all those pretty things on it?" asked Ah Ping.

There were gifts for all, but never did any gift bring such rapture as the doll that was given to Ah Ping. In the innermost recesses of her heart she had always longed for one, and it would have brought tears to the eyes of the most hardened person to have seen the poor thin arms clasping it, and the pale, sad face lighting up with budding mother love.

Louey Ching, who had been guided by the Christmas Star, held closely her wonderful *goon jai*, which had come from the "tree of heaven," and gazed with understanding at the radiance; but Ah Ping, who for the first time saw it, pointed her finger to it and said:

"It is so beautiful. What is it?" and Mama replied, with tears of gratitude in her eyes:

"It is the Star of Bethlehem, Ah Ping, and it has guided you both into the haven of peace."

CHAPTER NINETEEN

A LITTLE CHINESE REFUGEE

STANDING in a doorway, the lady had waited long before she saw a highbinder leave the door opposite, and go up the slanting streets of Chinatown. She was not afraid of him, for she feared nothing, but thought it best to make this first call without his knowledge.

Ah Gum and his little brother Ah Sing stood outside the door, and were to give the lady a signal if they saw him returning. They had known and loved her a long time, and, indeed, it was through a secret that Ah Gum had told her that she had found out something—something which had made her come

"Ah Gum and his little brother, Ah Sing, stood outside the door."

to this place to-day, and ascend an evil-looking stairway until she came to a certain room. Here she paused a moment, as if listening. She could hear a child's voice, but it had not the sound of a happy voice. The lady, with the far-seeing eyes of love, hoped the day would come when it would be happy, and would have a child's joyous heart back of it. It was to be her duty and pleasure to make it so.

Hesitating no longer, she now spoke through the small aperture in the door, saying:

"I am a good friend; one who loves the Chinese people. I would like to see the lady, please!" It would not be wise to say that she wanted to see the *mooie jai*, for that would thwart her plans at the outset.

A Chinese woman opened the door cautiously. Such a sweet, smiling face as this lady brought with her must surely bring its reward, even in heathen quarters, and this time the reward was that the door was opened, and she was allowed to enter.

Instinctively she felt the presence of some one else in the room. The little some one was crouching timidly, Chinese fashion, behind a screen, and the lady was not supposed to see, but she did. She had a way of seeing things, but always knew what to do about it; and so, just at the proper moment, she glanced at the child and smiled, while she said, "O, is this your little girl?" The woman said, "Yes," which was not true, of course, but the lady pretended to believe her.

The timid little slave did not know whether to come forward or not, as it was the place of a slave to keep always in the background; but the lady held out her hands, and said to her, "Come to me, *ah mooie*, I love little girls."

The child could not resist this appeal, and, glancing apprehensively at the sullen face of her mistress, she crept quietly to the lady's side, and into the arms which always had room for a Chinese slave.

The lady knew that if the child had really been the daughter of this rich woman she would not have been garbed in plain black sateen, but on this occasion (for it was a feast day) would have worn gay silks, and all the bright finery with which a Chinese mother loves to deck her child. There was nothing to do this time except to become friends with the sour-faced mistress, so that she might be invited to come again. Just one more time would be sufficient, she thought.

To the slave child, Ah Ging, the bare room seemed transformed, and she forgot for awhile that she was only a worthless slave, and would in all probability be beaten for being happy for a few moments. She forgot all that, after the manner of children, and only remembered that this lady had a wonderful watch and chain—a watch that would tick and seem alive, and would open its glittering lids and show—what? Why, the sweet face of a little Chinese girl; a girl who was gorgeously arrayed, and had jewels in her hair and in her ears; a girl who looked so very happy that Ah Ging said aloud, "The gel (girl) he look happy—no look solly—I think he got mama!"

It was so pathetic to see the longing for mother love thus innocently expressed, that the lady had to turn away and look out on the balcony, and blink awfully hard. One tear got away, though, and fell right on the toil-worn fingers of the little slave, who looked up in surprise. She did not know the cause of the tear, but somehow it brought the two very close together, and the child forgot the presence of her cruel mistress, and only remembered that she loved to hold the warm, soft hands of her new friend. Lovingly she fingered the material of the lady's dress, and admired the neat shirtwaist, and the hat with the pretty flowers; but most of all she loved the watch.

And now the lady moved toward the balcony, where she could look down on another one, and on the heads of Ah Gum and Ah Sing, who were still at their post. This new friend wanted to discover all the ins and outs of the place, if she could, as there might be a day when she would need to understand all. She realized, however, that she must not stay too long, as the highbinder might return at any moment; so, clasping the child's hand, she at last said good-bye, telling them she would soon come again.

The two big round lanterns seemed to smile at her as she stepped into the slanting streets again, and Ah Gum said, "I glad you come; I heap scare the man look see you—he no good—he not Clistian!" No, he was not a Christian, unless that meant going once a month to the temple of Lung Gong, and bowing his heathen head, and then returning to beat the little slave who did all the work for himself and his sullen wife.

Oftentimes the child had almost hoped that some day a big dragon would kill them. She dared not, however, dwell on this very much, lest she should be tempted to pray for it, and that would be wrong, for even slaves may have their ideas of what is right and wrong.

That was a festal night in Chinatown, and it was the duty of the slave to arrange for the midnight feast, the offerings on the table. The master and mistress in their rich festival attire would then proceed to worship, while the air would be heavy with the incense smoke, which seemed to the child as if it tried to kill the delicate fragrance of the almond spray which she had so lovingly placed in the vase. It also seemed to her that the almond petals leaned down and whispered

"The master and mistress in their rich festival attire would then proceed to worship."

to the Chinese lilies and said, "Why can't the master and his wife be good and pure, as we are? Why are they so wicked and ugly, when they might be sweet and fragrant?" This child, who had herself a lily's white heart, always seemed to understand the message of the blossoms.

She was not beaten to-night, after all. Perhaps they forgot, or—perhaps they were afraid of the gods, and refrained from beating her on a feast day. She did not care what the reason was. She cared for nothing to-night, because in her poor starved heart the bird of love was singing, and she knew—she knew, that she had found a friend.

When all were asleep, a strange thought came to her. It was—why not run away from the cruel master, and find the good lady with the watch? It would be very easy, for surely there could not be two good ladies with watches. But how could she run away? The door was always locked; of course it would be locked now. She would again go and see, as she had done so many times before, only to meet with disappointment. With bare feet she slipped cautiously to the door, softly turned the knob, and—it opened!

She had dreamed it, of course. It could not be true, for she had had this same dream many times. She began to rub her eyes, but the spring breeze from the outer world entered and caressed her lovingly, almost as the soft hands of the lady had done; and she knew she had not dreamed. She did not stop to wonder why, or she would have known that her ignorant heathen master had left it unfastened so that the spirits of his departed ancestors might the more easily come in and partake of the feast on the table.

Slipping a warm *sohm* over the one she wore at night, and taking her sandals in her hand, Ah Ging crept out into the night, and into freedom. "I will walk until I find the lady with the pretty watch," she said to herself. "Perhaps she will let me work for her, and I know—I know, she will not beat me."

She grew very tired, and the cobbles hurt her feet, while the darkness seemed full of evil. She was oppressed with the thought that something unusual was about to happen, and at last sat down, too weary to proceed further, right on the doorsill of one of the fashionable shops on Kearney Street—and away from the great Chinese quarter. She was soon asleep, and dreaming of the one she had once called father. Her mother had died, but she and her father had loved each other so, and had been very happy together in China, until—she was stolen one night, and taken away, and the loving father never knew where she had gone.

And so the little slave dreamed on, to be

rudely awakened, a thousand times more rudely even, than her old mistress had ever awakened her, by something—a terrible SOMETHING—she knew not what. She only knew that she was being violently shaken and beaten from side to side of the great doorway.

All around her she could hear an awful crashing and rumbling, and the tall buildings were swaying like reeds in a wind. It must be because she had run away, and the gods were angry about it. The very earth seemed each moment as if it would open and swallow her up.

In the gray light some one came running past the doorway where she sat. This some one was Chinese, and the child cried aloud to him in agony, "O, please—PLEASE tell Di See (the devil) to stop! I will go back and be beaten again, if only he will stop!" Something familiar in the tones of the childish voice made the frightened man pause, even more frightened than before, for this seemed a voice from the dead.

It sounded like—like—"*Ah Ging*! *samen jai—gum fah!*" (Ah Ging! my child—golden flower!") he cried, and amid the toppling ruins, and in the very face of death, love found its own. The heartbroken father had discovered his child, although he knew not at that dreadful moment how long he could keep her, for it seemed then that neither of them could escape from this terrible thing. With a sob of mingled joy and terror the child threw herself into her father's arms, crying, "*Mea wah? mea wah?*" (what is it?) "It must be the end of the world!" he replied, holding her tightly to his breast. "It seems too terrible for an earthquake."

No one noticed the Chinese child, although the streets were crowded with people, for all had one thought—to flee from this thing, whatever it was; to run away from the big, beautiful city which was soon to be a blackened mass of ruins, and to get out into the hills and fields, with no covering save the sky.

Realizing that he had no time to waste, the father now grasped his child by the hand, saying, "*Ah mooie*, we must run! we must not stay here and die." Fear lent wings to their feet, until at last, exhausted, they reached the ferry building, and were hustled on board a big boat, crowded with frightened people, running away from it all.

That night they slept in the streets of Oakland, with thousands of other Chinese people, but they did not see the cruel master and mistress.

When darkness fell upon them they huddled up together, and saw the great and beautiful city of San Francisco hurl its red banners of flame against the sky and go down to destruction.

And the child knew that the Red Dragon had destroyed the picturesque Chinatown, and the idols in all the homes and temples.

In her little heathen heart she felt nothing but kindness for the two who had been so unkind to her.

CHAPTER TWENTY

HOW THE MOOIE JAI FLED FROM THE RED DRAGON

THE *mooie jai*, big and little, were making great preparations for a meeting which was to be held next day in the Rescue Home. All worked willingly and gladly, for they wished people to see how beautiful their Home was, and how daintily it was tended.

At last good-night was said, and the large family were wrapped in peaceful slumber, only to be rudely awakened by the terrible earthquake shock, which will never be forgotten in the world's history. There was a great fear among the seventy girls in the Mission, but none thought of her own safety alone,

"No more 'devil parades' and silk-gowned priests."

but also of the safety of some one else, and the older girls showed a mother's tenderness and consideration for the tots.

It was really marvelous that this five-story brick building on the steep side of a sandhill could have been kept from falling to pieces, and crushing all the girls, but the God to whom these dear rescued heathen girls had so many times prayed was in it all; and now His protecting love overshadowed the place.

Soon wreaths of smoke rose in all directions, and, like a great dragon, enveloped the whole city with a thousand tongues of flame, destroying the famed San Francisco and its mysterious and wonderful Chinatown. No more "devil parades" and silk-gowned priests; gone were the rich balconies, with their burden of pretty Chinese women and children; gone the radiant rows of scintillating *joss* lanterns; gone the richly-furnished *joss* houses with their gods of clay, and the shops filled with rarest works of art from Oriental climes. Nothing—no matter how beautiful and how priceless—could stand before the cruel breath of the Red Dragon.

But even in the midst of terror one must eat, and so the matron and older girls began to think about feeding all the hungry ones. How to cook without any chimney was indeed a problem, and that idea had to be given up; but almost before the shock was over, the matron had thought of this, and procured from a nearby bakery a large basket of bread. There were plenty of apples, too, and best of all was the quantity of hot tea, always loved by the Chinese, but surely never so acceptable as now, when all were hungry and weak and cold.

For the last time the girls gathered around the table and sang; then they repeated the Twenty-third Psalm, which had never appealed to them as it did now, nor had such depths of meaning. "For Thou art with me" seemed to ring in their ears, and to follow and protect them. Before, these had been mere words, but now they were alive and tangible, and even the rescued slaves wondered how it fared at such a time with those who did not believe in any God.

While the simple meal was in progress another terrible shock came, and as they ran to the doors and windows and looked out they saw that the thin wreaths of smoke had grown to ominous proportions, and had blotted out the blue sky and the dimpling bay, and there was no more brightness anywhere. As they gazed with horror at the scene, a troop of United States cavalry galloped past at full speed. The city was under martial law! What were they to do? Things surely could not be much worse.

While they were trying to think of some plan, there came their good angel, in the form of the family physician, who, without her own breakfast, had walked a long distance to see if the girls were safe. The smaller ones, each carrying some treasure, were sent home with her, and that burden was lifted for a time.

At last it was decided to rest that night in a church at the corner of Van Ness Avenue, as the fire was not near it at the time.

On all sides could now be seen crowds of frightened people, heathen and Christian, huddling in the streets, all together, and no one stopped then to inquire who was white and who was yellow, for the Red Dragon pursued all alike, and preacher and heathen priest were all one.

Such a time of terror brings out the best in every human soul, and all hearts were overflowing with love.

Early the next morning the little band went back to try and gather up some of their treasures before the fire should come. At first the soldiers refused to allow this, but one, with a sympathetic heart, finally turned his back, while they ran in and hastily collected the most necessary things.

How Miss Cameron's heart ached as she stood in the dear old place and saw all about her loved articles, around each one of which clustered such tender memories. Must she leave them to be devoured by the cruel Red Dragon? Yes! there was no way to save everything, so, hastily snatching some valuables and papers, she loaded each girl like a little pack mule, and prepared for the long march.

"What shall we take? What shall we leave?" all inquired. Strips of sheet were used for rope, and broom sticks for poles, and thus large bundles were carried by each girl. They had to laugh, amid all the sadness, to see how much they resembled Chinese vegetable peddlers.

One of the older girls had a box of love letters in her bundle, and felt so genuinely distressed over leaving it that she was finally given permission to carry it with her.

The young mothers strapped their babies to their backs, Indian fashion, while the others carried the bedding for them. Of what use were tears, after all? It was much better to laugh, and so laugh they did, for the Chinese are always ready for a giggle, even through ruin and desolation, and though scorched with the hot breath of the Red Dragon.

It was a long walk to the ferry, but this was at last reached, and they took a steamer for San Anselmo, across the bay. Exhausted, they sank down on the lower deck, mid babies and bundles, tired and homeless, but not unhappy.

A few days after this the Lady of Love happened to be in Oakland, going about among the Chinese refugees.

After the Red Dragon came.

Ah Ging, who had found her father in the earthquake, was there, and still remembered.

"I wish—O, I wish—" she was saying, "I could find the lady with the pretty watch!" and then—

O, wonder of wonders! Some one was lifting her up from the hard ground, and this time some one had tears—real tears—unmistakable tears—in her eyes, and did not try to hide them. Clasping the cold hands in her own warm ones, she said, "Little one, are you all alone?" and the child replied, "No! no! the carthklakc he find my papa! Now I velly happy! I no more solly!"

Finding that the father could speak English, the lady now talked to him, and explained how she had intended to rescue the little slave, and said also that she had had a Rescue Home for Chinese slave girls, and had escaped with them all to San Rafael. How very happy she was when the father told her he would like to have the child put into her care, to be educated. Ah Ging's cup of joy was now filled to overflowing, and they all went to San Rafael, where she found the jolliest, happiest crowd of girls that one would care to see. It did not take her long to find the one whose pretty face was in the lady's watch, and they soon became great friends.

The father found employment in San Rafael, where he could see his child every day, and as he left he whispered something in her ear which made her forget all her troubles at once, and she gave a real, genuine child's squeal.

The secret he whispered was, "When Chinese New Year comes, I will give you a watch that ticks, and I will have in it—the Lady's picture!"

*"The new Home stands where it did before—
dauntless and brave."*

CHAPTER TWENTY-ONE

INTO THE LIGHT

SPRING is in the land—spring, who scatters over the brown earth her fragrant message of love, and clothes the bare hills with a tender robe of green.

The blue bay lies peaceful—quiescent—under April's tender smile, while the white ships cover its broad bosom, as in the dear old days. The blue bay rejoices in the fact that San Francisco is reborn—Chinatown is reborn—the Home is reborn. Now, in the glad Easter time, the Home stands where it did before, dauntless and brave, as if in defiance of destruction, and saying to the suffering ones:

"Once inside my strong arms you are safe;

for here you will find peace, and the world—the wicked part of it—can not enter."

* * * * *

The dedication is going on, and people from all corners of the earth are there to add their encouraging words. The place is crowded with visitors, and the girls are welcoming them all with characteristic sweetness of manner.

The furnishings are Oriental, and the air is fragrant with flowers.

"The Tiger," very proud and very happy, seems to be everywhere at once. If she goes to her room, thinking to rest a few moments, there is soon a voice at the door calling, "Mama!" and she always opens the door and soothes the wound, whether it be a cut on the finger or a stab in the heart. The very air is full of love.

And away up on the roof is a garden, with

real flowers and real sunshine, for the ones who have never known flowers and sunshine. Up here among the blossoms one is safe, for here never a highbinder can find his way.

And the girls—how they have all unfolded and blossomed out in the atmosphere of love!

To-night the air is full of mystery—delightful mystery. In one of the rooms a radiantly beautiful girl leans from the window in one last reverie of maidenhood, and gazes at the picturesque Chinatown, once fraught with unhappiness for her, but now only beautiful.

Everywhere the dragon lanterns are swaying and shining. Away back in one corner of her heart she still almost believes that they are inhabited by good fairies. As she leans and gazes, she now realizes that she will no more enter the upside-down country, for she has come into that pleasing land where everything is pleasantness and peace.

She can not stay long in this girlish reverie, however, for soon she feels a tender touch on her hand, and with radiant face she looks into the love-lit eyes of—the Lantern Friend!

The hour has come!

Ah Ching must now go down into the chapel and be the first bride of the new Home.

According to the bride's request, there is a huge lantern made of pure white roses, and under this, stand Ah Ching—herself as sweet and pure as the roses—and the man she loves, the friend the lanterns sent.

Mama is trying hard to keep back the tears and present a brave face to the world, but Ah Ching has taken such a firm hold on her heart strings that it is hard to give her up. Ah Ching herself dares not look at Mama during the brief ceremony, but keeps her eyes modestly down.

INTO THE LIGHT

Just as are pronounced the last words which have joined two loving hearts, some of the white rose petals drift down upon their closed hands, and Ah Ching is sure—sure—that a voice from out the big lantern whispers:

"You *have* come up into the light, my dear little slave.

www.ingramcontent.com/pod-product-compliance
Lightning Source LLC
LaVergne TN
LVHW011200110826
845150LV00006B/1279

* 9 7 8 1 4 2 5 5 7 2 7 8 5 *